♍   THE VIRGO ENIGMA   ♍

Cracking the Code

ALSO BY JANE RIDDER-PATRICK

A Handbook of Medical Astrology
Shaping Your Future (Series of 12 titles)
Shaping Your Relationships (Series of 12 titles)

The Zodiac Code series

THE
VIRGO
ENIGMA

Cracking the Code

JANE RIDDER-PATRICK

MAINSTREAM
PUBLISHING
EDINBURGH AND LONDON

For my son Max, with love

First published in Great Britain in 2004 by
MAINSTREAM PUBLISHING COMPANY
(EDINBURGH) LTD
7 Albany Street
Edinburgh EH1 3UG

ISBN 1 84018 531 7

A catalogue record for this book is available
from the British Library

Typeset in Allise and Van Dijck

Printed in Great Britain by
Antony Rowe Ltd., Chippenham, Wiltshire

ᚍ

ᚍ

around us. It gives us a language and a framework to examine and describe – quite literally – *anything* under the Sun, from countries to companies, from money markets to medical matters. Its most common application, however, is in helping people to understand themselves better using their own unique birth charts. Astrology has two main functions. One is to describe the traits and tendencies of whatever it is that is being examined, whether this is a state, a software company or someone's psyche. The other is to give an astonishingly accurate timetable for important changes within that entity. In the chapters that follow, we'll be using astrology to investigate the psychology of the innermost part of your personality, taking a look at what drives, inspires and motivates you.

Astrology uses an ancient system of symbols to describe profound truths about the nature of life on earth, truths that cannot be weighed and measured, but ones we recognise nevertheless, and that touch and move us at a deep level. By linking mythology and mathematics, astrology bridges the gap between our inner lives and our outer experiences, between mind and matter, between poetry and science.

Fate and Free Will

Some people think that astrology is all about foretelling the future, the implication being that everything is predestined and that we have no say in how our lives take shape. None of that is true. We are far from being helpless victims of fate. Everything that happens to us at any given time is the result of past choices. These choices may have been our own, or made by other people. They could even have been made long ago before we, or even our grandparents, were born. It is not always possible to prevent processes that

Contents

The 10 symbols on the inside of the chart wheel are the **PLANET** glyphs (see below)

The 12 symbols in the rim of the chart are the **SIGNS OF THE ZODIAC** (see below)

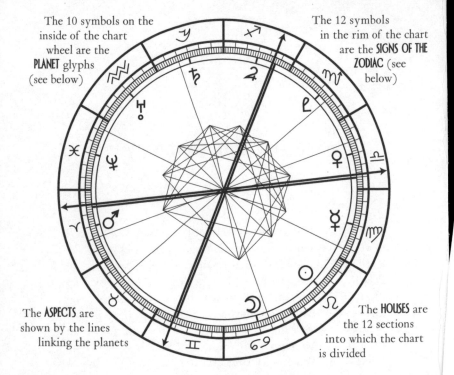

The **ASPECTS** are shown by the lines linking the planets

The **HOUSES** are the 12 sections into which the chart is divided

A Sample Birth Chart

Sign	Ruler	Sign	Ruler
Aries ♈	Mars ♂	Libra ♎	Venus ♀
Taurus ♉	Venus ♀	Scorpio ♏	Pluto ♇
Gemini ♊	Mercury ☿	Sagittarius ♐	Jupiter ♃
Cancer ♋	Moon ☽	Capricorn ♑	Saturn ♄
Leo ♌	Sun ☉	Aquarius ♒	Uranus ♅
Virgo ♍	Mercury ☿	Pisces ♓	Neptune ♆

ONE

The Truth of Astrology

MOST PEOPLE'S FIRST EXPERIENCE OF ASTROLOGY IS THROUGH newspapers and magazines. This is a mixed blessing for astrology's reputation – writing an astrology column to any degree of accuracy is a tough, many would say impossible, challenge. The astrologer has to try to say something meaningful about conditions that affect every single person belonging to the same sign, over a very short period of time, in a scant handful of words. The miracle is that some talented astrologers do manage to get across a tantalising whiff of the real thing and keep readers coming back for more of what most of us are hungry for – self-knowledge and reassurance about the future. The downside of the popularity of these columns is that many people think that all astrology is a branch of the entertainment industry and is limited to light-hearted fortune-telling. This is far from the truth.

What Astrology Can Offer

Serious astrology is one of the most sophisticated tools available to help us understand ourselves and the world

7

were set in motion in the past from coming to their logical conclusions as events that we then have to deal with. We are, however, all free to decide how to react to whatever is presented to us at every moment of our lives.

Your destiny is linked directly with your personality because the choices you make, consciously or unconsciously, depend largely on your own natural inclinations. It is these inclinations that psychological astrology describes. You can live out every single part of your chart in a constructive or a less constructive way. For instance, if you have Aries strong in your chart, action and initiative will play a major role in your life. It is your choice whether you express yourself aggressively or assertively, heroically or selfishly, and also whether you are the doer or the done-to. Making the right choices is important because every decision has consequences – and what you give out, sooner or later, you get back. If you don't know and understand yourself, you are 'fated' to act according to instinct and how your life experiences have conditioned you. By revealing how you are wired up temperamentally, astrology can highlight alternatives to blind knee-jerk reactions, which often make existing problems worse. This self-knowledge can allow you to make more informed free-will choices, and so help you create a better and more successful future for yourself.

Astrology and Prediction

Astrology cannot predict specific events based on your birth chart. That kind of prediction belongs to clairvoyance and divination. These specialities, when practised by gifted and responsible individuals, can give penetrating insights into events that are likely to happen in the future if matters proceed along their present course.

The real benefit of seeing into the future is that if we don't like what could happen if we carry on the way we're going, we can take steps either to prevent it or to lessen its impact. Rarely is the future chiselled out in stone. There are many possible futures. What you feed with your attention grows. Using your birth chart, a competent astrologer can map out, for years in advance, major turning points, showing which areas of your life will be affected at these times and the kind of change that will be taking place. This information gives answers to the questions that most clients ask in one way or another: 'Why me, why this and why now?' If you accept responsibility for facing what needs to be done at the appropriate time, and doing it, you can change the course of your life for the better.

Astrology and the Soul

What is sometimes called the soul and its purpose is a mystery much more profound than astrology. Most of us have experienced 'chance' meetings and apparent 'tragedies' which have affected the direction of our entire lives. There is an intelligence at work that is infinitely wiser and more powerful than the will or wishes of our small egocentric personalities. This force, whatever name we give it – Universal Wisdom, the Inner Guide, the Self, a guardian angel – steers us into exactly the right conditions for our souls' growth. Astrology can pinpoint the turning points in the course of your destiny and describe the equipment that you have at your disposal for serving, or resisting, the soul's purpose. That equipment is your personality.

Who Are You?

You are no doubt aware of your many good qualities as well as your rather more resistible ones that you might prefer to

ONE

The Truth of Astrology

MOST PEOPLE'S FIRST EXPERIENCE OF ASTROLOGY IS THROUGH newspapers and magazines. This is a mixed blessing for astrology's reputation – writing an astrology column to any degree of accuracy is a tough, many would say impossible, challenge. The astrologer has to try to say something meaningful about conditions that affect every single person belonging to the same sign, over a very short period of time, in a scant handful of words. The miracle is that some talented astrologers do manage to get across a tantalising whiff of the real thing and keep readers coming back for more of what most of us are hungry for – self-knowledge and reassurance about the future. The downside of the popularity of these columns is that many people think that all astrology is a branch of the entertainment industry and is limited to light-hearted fortune-telling. This is far from the truth.

What Astrology Can Offer

Serious astrology is one of the most sophisticated tools available to help us understand ourselves and the world around us. It gives us a language and a framework to examine and describe – quite literally – *anything* under the Sun, from countries to companies, from money markets to medical matters. Its most common application, however, is in helping people to understand themselves better using their own unique birth charts. Astrology has two main functions. One is to describe the traits and tendencies of whatever it is that is being examined, whether this is a state, a software company or someone's psyche. The other is to give an astonishingly accurate timetable for important changes within that entity. In the chapters that follow, we'll be using astrology to investigate the psychology of the innermost part of your personality, taking a look at what drives, inspires and motivates you.

Astrology uses an ancient system of symbols to describe profound truths about the nature of life on earth, truths that cannot be weighed and measured, but ones we recognise nevertheless, and that touch and move us at a deep level. By linking mythology and mathematics, astrology bridges the gap between our inner lives and our outer experiences, between mind and matter, between poetry and science.

Fate and Free Will

Some people think that astrology is all about foretelling the future, the implication being that everything is predestined and that we have no say in how our lives take shape. None of that is true. We are far from being helpless victims of fate. Everything that happens to us at any given time is the result of past choices. These choices may have been our own, or made by other people. They could even have been made long ago before we, or even our grandparents, were born. It is not always possible to prevent processes that

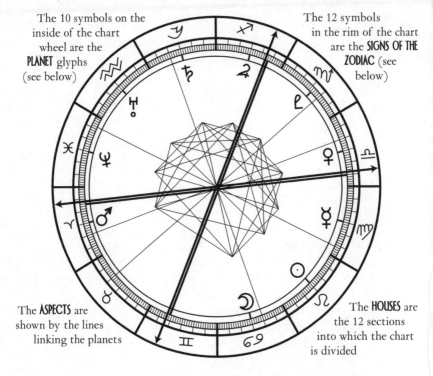

The 10 symbols on the inside of the chart wheel are the **PLANET** glyphs (see below)

The 12 symbols in the rim of the chart are the **SIGNS OF THE ZODIAC** (see below)

The **ASPECTS** are shown by the lines linking the planets

The **HOUSES** are the 12 sections into which the chart is divided

A Sample Birth Chart

Sign		Ruler		Sign		Ruler	
Aries	♈	Mars	♂	Libra	♎	Venus	♀
Taurus	♉	Venus	♀	Scorpio	♏	Pluto	♇
Gemini	♊	Mercury	☿	Sagittarius	♐	Jupiter	♃
Cancer	♋	Moon	☽	Capricorn	♑	Saturn	♄
Leo	♌	Sun	☉	Aquarius	♒	Uranus	♅
Virgo	♍	Mercury	☿	Pisces	♓	Neptune	♆

Contents

were set in motion in the past from coming to their logical conclusions as events that we then have to deal with. We are, however, all free to decide how to react to whatever is presented to us at every moment of our lives.

Your destiny is linked directly with your personality because the choices you make, consciously or unconsciously, depend largely on your own natural inclinations. It is these inclinations that psychological astrology describes. You can live out every single part of your chart in a constructive or a less constructive way. For instance, if you have Aries strong in your chart, action and initiative will play a major role in your life. It is your choice whether you express yourself aggressively or assertively, heroically or selfishly, and also whether you are the doer or the done-to. Making the right choices is important because every decision has consequences – and what you give out, sooner or later, you get back. If you don't know and understand yourself, you are 'fated' to act according to instinct and how your life experiences have conditioned you. By revealing how you are wired up temperamentally, astrology can highlight alternatives to blind knee-jerk reactions, which often make existing problems worse. This self-knowledge can allow you to make more informed free-will choices, and so help you create a better and more successful future for yourself.

Astrology and Prediction

Astrology cannot predict specific events based on your birth chart. That kind of prediction belongs to clairvoyance and divination. These specialities, when practised by gifted and responsible individuals, can give penetrating insights into events that are likely to happen in the future if matters proceed along their present course.

The real benefit of seeing into the future is that if we don't like what could happen if we carry on the way we're going, we can take steps either to prevent it or to lessen its impact. Rarely is the future chiselled out in stone. There are many possible futures. What you feed with your attention grows. Using your birth chart, a competent astrologer can map out, for years in advance, major turning points, showing which areas of your life will be affected at these times and the kind of change that will be taking place. This information gives answers to the questions that most clients ask in one way or another: 'Why me, why this and why now?' If you accept responsibility for facing what needs to be done at the appropriate time, and doing it, you can change the course of your life for the better.

Astrology and the Soul

What is sometimes called the soul and its purpose is a mystery much more profound than astrology. Most of us have experienced 'chance' meetings and apparent 'tragedies' which have affected the direction of our entire lives. There is an intelligence at work that is infinitely wiser and more powerful than the will or wishes of our small egocentric personalities. This force, whatever name we give it – Universal Wisdom, the Inner Guide, the Self, a guardian angel – steers us into exactly the right conditions for our souls' growth. Astrology can pinpoint the turning points in the course of your destiny and describe the equipment that you have at your disposal for serving, or resisting, the soul's purpose. That equipment is your personality.

Who Are You?

You are no doubt aware of your many good qualities as well as your rather more resistible ones that you might prefer to keep firmly under wraps. Maybe you have wondered why it is that one part of your personality seems to want to do one thing while another part is stubbornly intent on doing the exact opposite. Have you ever wished that you could crack the code that holds the secrets of what makes you – and significant others – behave in the complex way you do? The good news is that you can, with the help of your astrological birth chart, sometimes known as your horoscope.

Just as surely as your DNA identifies you and distinguishes you from everyone else, as well as encoding your peculiarities and potential, your birth chart reveals the unique 'DNA fingerprinting' of your personality. This may seem a staggering claim, but it is one that those who have experienced serious astrology will endorse, so let's take a closer look at what a birth chart is.

Your Birth Chart

Your birth chart is a simplified diagram of the positions of the planets, as seen from the place of your birth, at the moment you took your first independent breath. Critics have said that astrology is obviously nonsense because birth charts are drawn up as if the Sun and all the planets moved round the Earth.

We know in our minds that the Earth moves round the Sun, but that doesn't stop us seeing the Sun rise in the east in the morning and move across the sky to set in the west in the evening. This is an optical illusion. In the same way, we know (or at least most of us know) that we are not really the centre of the universe, but that doesn't stop us experiencing ourselves as being at the focal point of our own personal worlds. It is impossible to live life in any other way. It is the strength, not weakness, of astrology that it describes from your own unique viewpoint how you, as an individual, experience life.

Erecting Your Chart

To draw up a full birth chart you need three pieces of information – the date, time and place of your birth. With your birth date alone you can find the positions of all the planets (except sometimes the Moon) to a good enough degree of accuracy to reveal a great deal of important information about you. If you have the time and place of birth, too, an astrologer can calculate your Ascendant or Rising Sign and the houses of your chart – see below. The Ascendant is a bit like the front door of your personality and describes your general outlook on life. (If you know your Ascendant sign, you might like to read more about its characteristics in the book on that sign in this series.)

The diagram on page 6 shows what a birth chart looks like. Most people find it pretty daunting at first sight but it actually breaks down into only four basic units – the planets, the signs, the aspects and the houses.

The Planets

Below is a simple list of what the planets represent.

PLANET	REPRESENTS YOUR URGE TO
☉ The Sun	express your identity
☽ The Moon	feel nurtured and safe
☿ Mercury	make connections
♀ Venus	attract what you love
♂ Mars	assert your will
♃ Jupiter	find meaning in life
♄ Saturn	achieve your ambitions
♅ Uranus	challenge tradition
♆ Neptune	serve an ideal
♇ Pluto	eliminate, transform and survive

The planets represent the main psychological drives that every single one of us has. The exact way in which we express these drives is not fixed from birth but develops and evolves throughout our lives, both consciously and unconsciously. In this book we will be examining in detail four of these planets – your Sun, Moon, Mercury and Venus. These are the bodies that are right at the heart of our solar system. They correspond, in psychological astrology, to the core of your personality and represent how you express yourself, what motivates you emotionally, how you use your mind and what brings you pleasure.

The Signs
The signs your planets are in show how you tend to express your inner drives. For example, if your Mars is in the action sign of Aries, you will assert yourself pretty directly, pulling no punches. If your Venus is in secretive Scorpio, you will attract, and also be attracted to, emotionally intense relationships. There is a summary of all of the signs on p. 128.

The Aspects
Aspects are important relationships between planets and whether your inner characteristics clash with or complement each other depends largely on whether or not they are in aspect and whether that aspect is an easy or a challenging one. In Chapter Six we'll be looking at some challenging aspects to the Sun.

The Houses
Your birth chart is divided into 12 slices, called houses, each of which is associated with a particular area of life, such as friendships, travel or home life. If, for example, you have your Uranus in the house of career, you are almost

certainly a bit of a maverick at work. If you have your Neptune in the house of partnership, you are likely to idealise your husband, wife or business partner.

The Nature of Time

Your birth chart records a moment in time and space, like a still from a movie – the movie being the apparent movement of the planets round the earth. We all know that time is something that can be measured in precise units, which are always the same, like seconds, months and centuries. But if you stop to reflect for a moment, you'll also recognise that time doesn't always feel the same. Twenty minutes waiting for a bus on a cold, rainy day can seem like a miserable eternity, while the same amount of time spent with someone you love can pass in a flash. As Einstein would say – that's relativity.

There are times in history when something significant seems to be in the air, but even when nothing momentous is happening the quality of time shifts into different 'moods' from moment to moment. Your birth chart is impregnated with the qualities of the time when you were born. For example, people who were born in the mid-to-late 1960s, when society was undergoing major disruptive changes, carry those powerful energies within them and their personalities reflect, in many ways, the turmoil of those troubled and exciting times. Now, as adults, the choices that those individuals make, based on their own inner conflicts and compulsions, will help shape the future of society for better or worse. And so it goes on through the generations.

Seed Meets Soil

There is no such thing as a good or bad chart, nor is any one sign better or worse than another. There are simply 12 different, but equally important, life focuses. It's useful to keep in mind the fact that the chart of each one of us is made up of all the signs of the zodiac. This means that we'll act out, or experience, *every* sign somewhere in our lives. It is true, however, that some individual charts are more challenging than others; but the greater the challenge, the greater the potential for achievement and self-understanding.

In gardening terms, your chart is a bit like the picture on a seed packet. It shows what you could become. If the seeds are of poppies, there's no way you'll get petunias, but external conditions will affect how they grow. With healthy soil, a friendly climate and green-fingered gardeners, the plants have an excellent chance of flourishing. With poor soil, a harsh climate or constant neglect, the seeds will be forced to struggle. This is not always a disadvantage. They can become hardy and adapt, finding new and creative ways of evolving and thriving under more extreme conditions than the plant that was well cared for. It's the same with your chart. The environment you were raised in may have been friendly or hostile to your nature and it will have done much to shape your life until now. Using the insights of astrology to affirm who you are, you can, as an adult, provide your own ideal conditions, become your own best gardener and live out more fully – and successfully – your own highest potential.

TWO

The Symbolism of Virgo

WE CAN LEARN A GREAT DEAL ABOUT A SIGN BY LOOKING at the symbolism and the myths and legends associated with it. These carry more information than plain facts alone and hint at the deeper meanings and significance of the sign.

The Virgo glyph looks like a letter 'M' with an extra loop tucked in neatly at the end. 'M' is said to represent many of the attributes and associations of Virgo – maiden, Mary, mind, Mercury, medicine, measuring and meticulousness.

Some interpret the glyph as the female sex organs, closed in the virginal state. Contrast this with the glyph for Scorpio, which is similar, but depicts masculine potency fully prepared for action. It is said that at one time there were only ten signs of the zodiac; Libra did not yet exist, and Virgo and Scorpio were combined. These two signs do share some common characteristics, such as a desire to penetrate to the heart of the matter and to eliminate non-essentials, but their motivations are quite different. Virgo is focused on effectiveness, while Scorpio is intent on survival.

The segments of the glyph can be seen as divisions, rather like the compartments of a filing cabinet, indicating the Virgo love of order and pointing to the way that you tend to break down every task into smaller manageable units so that they can be dealt with more easily. The 'M' shape can also represent the loops of the intestines, a part of the body associated with Virgo. In the small intestines food is split into its component parts. What is useful for the body is extracted and absorbed; the rest is sent on its way to be disposed of in the usual fashion – a fitting parallel to Virgo's analytical and efficient way of working.

The coils of the glyph also refer to the energy and power stored up in Virgo, potentially available for productive work, but shown locked in by the last sweep of the 'M' curled back on itself. This refers both to the self-contained nature of Virgo and to the fact that your energy needs to find a constructive outlet in the outer world or it can turn in on itself as debilitating nervous tension and destructive self-criticism.

Virgo the Maiden

The symbol for Virgo is the maiden, usually shown holding a sheaf of wheat or an ear of corn. These represent the ripe harvest, of both wisdom and material rewards, that Virgos can reap from practical experience. It also highlights Virgo's main focus, which is useful work. Since grain is almost inedible in its raw state, it needs to be stripped of its stalks and outer husks before it can be used for food – Virgos are adept at separating the chaff from the grain in any situation.

Virgo is often shown as an angel with wings. The sign is also associated with the Virgin Mary, whose role was to be a vehicle for giving form to the divine in the material world.

These images refer to Virgo's humility, love of simplicity and desire to be of service. The maiden represents potential, fertility and purity. Virgo, the virgin, has nothing to do with being sexually inexperienced. In ancient times, many virgin goddesses were far from celibate. The word virgin means not being owned or beholden to any man or master, but possessing a life of one's own. A virgin therefore is a woman — or man — not bound to the will of another by conventional constraints. It is essentially a sacred state, because she is then free to be psychically open to divine inspiration. Translated into psychology, that means that she is answerable only to her own conscience and inner authority in doing what she believes to be right. There's a part of Virgo, man or woman, that remains untouched and unavailable in even the most intimate of relationships. This is why some people may see you as rather reserved and can even accuse you of being selfish (in other words, not doing what they want you to!).

Virgo is the sixth sign of the Zodiac and, like the previous five, it is concerned with developing aspects of the individual. It is the most complete and self-contained of all the signs. From Libra on, each of the signs is then focused on relationships with others, and with the community.

The Ruler of Virgo

Virgo shares its ruling planet, Mercury, with Gemini. He was the god of commerce, connections and craftsmanship — as well as craftiness. Being resourceful, his skills lay in making deals and using his wit and intelligence to come up with ingenious solutions to difficult problems. Virgos tend to show more of the practical skills and inventiveness of Mercury, while in Gemini the go-between and mischief-loving aspects are usually more apparent.

Mercury is often seen with his magic wand, the caduceus. This is a wing-topped staff with two serpents twined around it, representing fertility, wisdom, healing and impartiality. Many medical organisations have incorporated the caduceus into their logo. Virgo is the sign of the mind–body connection and many Virgos are skilled healers, not only of ailing bodies and minds, but of anything in need of fixing, using both hands and mind to weave and mend, restoring order where previously there was disorder and chaos. Esoteric astrology says that the true ruler of Virgo is Vulcan, the smith god who was a skilled craftsman with a brilliant mind, and that the planet Vulcan will be discovered in the not-too-distant future.

The Season of Virgo

Virgo's season, in the northern hemisphere, is at the time of harvest, when the fruits of previous labours are being gathered in, ready to be processed and stored so that food will be available throughout the long winter to come. The availability and palatability of food depends on careful and often ingenious preparation and preservation. Any mistakes or carelessness at this time can mean the difference between hunger and sufficiency. No wonder Virgos are so concerned with getting right whatever they turn their hands – and minds – to.

THREE

The Heart of the Sun

THE GLYPH FOR THE SUN IS A PERFECT CIRCLE WITH A DOT in the centre and symbolises our dual nature – earthly and eternal. The circle stands for the boundary of the personality, which distinguishes and separates each individual from every other individual, for it is our differences from other people that make us unique, not our similarities. The dot in the centre indicates the mysterious 'divine spark' within us and the potential for becoming conscious of who we truly are, where we have come from and what we may become.

The Meaning of the Sun
Each of your planets represents a different strand of your personality. The Sun is often reckoned to be the most important factor of your whole birth chart. It describes your sense of identity, and the sign that the Sun was in when you were born, your Sun sign, along with its house position and any aspects to other planets, shows how you express and devlop that identity.

Your Role in Life

Each of the signs is associated with certain roles that can be played in an infinite number of ways. Take one of the roles of Aries, which is the warrior. A warrior can cover anything from Attila the Hun, who devastated vast stretches of Europe with his deliberate violence, to an eco-warrior, battling to save the environment. The role, warrior, is the same; the motivation and actions are totally different. You can live out every part of your personality in four main ways – as creator, destroyer, onlooker or victim. How you act depends on who you choose to be from the endless variations possible from the symbolism of each of your planets, but most particularly your Sun. And you do have a choice; not all Geminis are irresponsible space cadets nor is every Scorpio a sex-crazed sadist. This book aims to paint a picture of what some of your choices might be and show what choices, conscious or unconscious, some well-known people of your sign have made.

Your upbringing will have helped shape what you believe about yourself and out of those beliefs comes, automatically, behaviour to match. For example, if you believe you are a victim, you will behave like one and the world will happily oblige by victimising you. If you see yourself as a carer, life will present you with plenty to care for – and often to care about, too. If you identify yourself as an adventurer, you'll spot opportunities at every corner. If you're a winner, then you'll tend to succeed. Shift the way that you see yourself and your whole world shifts, too.

Your Vocation

Your Sun describes your major life focus. This is not always a career. As the poet Milton said: 'They also serve who only stand and wait.' It is impossible to tell from your Sun sign exactly what your calling is – there are people of all signs occupied in practically every area of life. What is important is not so much *what* you do, but the way that you do it and it is this – how you express yourself – that your Sun describes. If you spend most of your time working at an occupation or living in a situation where you can't give expression to the qualities of your Sun, or which forces you to go against the grain of your Sun's natural inclinations, then you're likely to live a life of quiet, or possibly even noisy, desperation.

On Whose Authority

Your personality, which your birth chart maps, is like a sensitive instrument that will resonate only to certain frequencies – those that are similar to its own. Your Sun shows the kind of authority that will strike a chord with you, either positively or negatively, because it is in harmony with yours. It can show how you relate to people in authority, especially your father. (It is the Moon that usually shows the relationship with your mother and home.) In adult life it can throw light onto the types of bosses you are likely to come across, and also how you could react to them. It is a major part of the maturing process to take responsibility for expressing your own authority wisely. When you do so, many of your problems with external authorities diminish or even disappear.

In a woman's chart the Sun can also describe the kind of husband she chooses. This is partly because, traditionally, a husband had legal authority over his wife. It is also because, especially in the early years of a marriage, many women choose to pour their energies into homemaking and supporting their husbands' work in the world, rather than their own, and so his career becomes her career. As a Virgo, you may find that your father, boss or husband shows either the positive or negative traits of Virgo or, as is usually the case, a mixture of both – hard-working, skilled and methodical or critical, stingy and an insufferable know-all.

Born on the Cusp
If you were born near the beginning or end of Virgo, you may know that your birthday falls on the cusp, or meeting point, of two signs. The Sun, however, can only be in one sign or the other. You can find out for sure which sign your Sun is in by checking the tables on pp. 97–8.

FOUR

The Drama of Being a Virgo

EACH SIGN IS ASSOCIATED WITH A CLUSTER OF ROLES THAT HAVE their own core drama or storyline. Being born is a bit like arriving in the middle of an ongoing play and slipping into a certain part. How we play our characters is powerfully shaped in early life by having to respond to the input of the other actors around us– the people that make up our families and communities. As the play of our lives unfolds, we usually become aware that there are themes which tend to repeat themselves. We may ask ourselves questions like 'Why do I always end up with all the work / caught up in fights / with partners who mistreat me / in dead-end jobs/ successful but unhappy . . .?' or whatever. Interestingly, I've found that people are less likely to question the wonderful things that happen to them again and again.

The good news is that once we recognise the way we have been playing our roles, we can then use our free-will choice to do some creative rescripting, using the same character in more constructive scenarios. Even better news is that if we change, the other people in our dramas have got to make some alterations, too. If you refuse to respond to the same old cues in the customary ways, they are going to have to get creative too.

A core role of Virgo is the craftsman, or craftswoman. There is something ritualistic about this kind of work when it is done properly. That may be why the sign of Virgo is associated with what has been called natural magic. This is simply another name for applying a working knowledge of the laws of nature to achieve some practical result. It is the direct ancestor of all of the arts and crafts, and of modern science and technology. A craftsman usually receives a commission because he or she has a reputation for having special talents and the ability to carry out skilful work. It is here that the ritual begins.

A ritual can be divided into four phases: intention, preparation, execution and completion. The first step is to make sure that there is clarity about what the intended outcome or end-product should be; leaving this undone can undermine the whole enterprise. Next comes the preparation stage, which is as much mental and spiritual as it is physical. A job that is not planned thoroughly will lead to inefficiency and a great deal of wasted effort. An old Chinese furniture-maker was once asked why he spent several days meditating before he even picked up a tool. He answered that he had to purify himself of every last trace of pride so as to be humble enough to listen to the guidance of the cosmos, through his intuition, without his ego getting in the way. That is Virgo at its highest. With the end in mind, the craftsman breaks the task down into its component parts and decides the order in which each step has to be done. She then draws up a list of materials needed, locates and assembles them and then lays them out neatly for maximal efficiency. To borrow from the marketing manager's slogan: success means having everything in the right place, at the right time, in the right quantity and at the right price.

The next stage – the creative work – requires skill, judgement and the ability to adapt and improvise, for it's rare that any undertaking runs smoothly from start to finish without a single hitch. Also, no matter how often a task has been done, there is almost always room for improvement and something new to be learned. A good craftsman works wonders within the clearly defined constraints of time and resources available. As the Virgo writer Goethe put it – it is when faced by limitations that true masters reveal themselves.

The end result of the labour for Virgo is, ideally, something that is functional but beautiful too – like the finest Shaker furniture. Craftsmen and women identify themselves with their work and, if they have any pride in themselves, they will not send out anything that is shoddy or flawed. They take quiet pleasure in receiving acknowledgement for work well done – especially from those who can recognise, and appreciate, quality. Then, after a short rest, it is on to the next task, and then the next one after that. It is in the creation of something worthwhile that a craftsman discovers his or her capabilities and takes immense satisfaction in the finished article as an expression of self and self-development. In the same way you, as a Virgo, order and improve yourself through ordering and improving the material world.

Other Virgo roles are the analyst, critic, editor, fixer, refiner and server. These too are tasks requiring skill, judgement and frequent responses and adjustments to the matter in hand.

How you choose to see your role will determine your behaviour. The following chapter describes some typical

Virgo behaviour. Remember, though, that there is no such thing as a person who is all Virgo and nothing but Virgo. You are much more complicated than that and other parts of your chart will modify, or may even seem to contradict, the single, but central, strand of your personality which is your Sun sign. These other sides of your nature will add colour and contrast and may restrict or reinforce your basic Virgo identity. They won't, however, cancel out the challenges you face as a Virgo.

FIVE

The Virgo Temperament

VIRGOS GET THE REPUTATION OF BEING FASTIDIOUSLY NEAT AND tidy. Sometimes this is true. The Belgian detective Hercule Poirot, created by Virgo crime writer Agatha Christie, was clearly born under the sign of the Hoover. Relentlessly fussy about his appearance, food and fads, he was forever brushing minute crumbs off everything in sight. By noticing tiny details and ordering his little grey cells to recall what was out of its usual place, he solved the most baffling of mysteries. It was reported that when Virgo actor Jeremy Irons found sticky floors and general grot at Shannon Airport, he picked up a mop and worked away quietly for half an hour, cleaning the place up, and felt much better afterwards. Another Virgo I know, when alone in public lavatories, finds clearing up the litter of loose tissues a therapeutic experience.

A quick survey, though, of friends and colleagues should soon disabuse you forever of the idea that all Virgos are duster-wielding, immaculately-groomed obsessives. Many are complete slobs in their dress and habits. Kitted out in sensible shoes and charity shop castoffs, the style image of some Virgo women is more Oxfemme than femme fatale.

Narrow Focus

The explanation lies in Virgo's tunnel vision. You pick out what is important to you from life's extensive menu and direct your attention towards that. Everything else is screened out. It makes you more effective and protects you from the sensory overload that could otherwise overwhelm you. So your life is, consciously or unconsciously, divided up into what you devote yourself to, and what you don't. If you see the point in dressing well, you'll do it superbly. If you don't, you'll plump for the purely functional and most cost efficient, sometimes with shuddersome consequences.

In your sharpness of focus, you can easily narrow yourself down to a tightly restricted range of interests. Like Martha in the Bible, who was too busy getting on with the housework to pay attention to epoch-making events going on around her, you are sometimes so intent on completing your tasks that you miss out on life's fun, beauty and drama. You are then in serious danger of becoming a workaholic – and remember: all work and no play makes Jack or Jill deadly dull. Work that demands a wide variety of skills and knowledge, plus friends who will lure you away from your duties at regular intervals, could save you from this dreary fate.

Full On

You prefer to work on one task until it is finished and you need enough time to do it properly, preferably uninterrupted. Too many distractions can leave you frazzled. This may be why many Virgos make reluctant parents. There are just too many simultaneous claims on your time and resources. You are usually good at saying 'no' to unwanted demands, but sometimes commitments won't allow for that. So, when you're under too much pressure and waves of anxiety tell you that you don't have the time, skill, energy or resources to do, and do properly, what needs to be done, your circuits may simply cut out. You may then develop physical symptoms forcing you to stop, or you could even do as Stephen Fry and Agatha Christie did at difficult times in their careers, which was simply to run for cover and disappear for a while. It's good to recognise when you're reaching your limit so that you can avoid being driven to such extremes.

What's the Use?

In any new situation you'll assess whether there's anything about it that could be put to good use and what could possibly grow out of it. Sunsets may delight you for ten minutes or so, then you'll start to get fidgety, for what can you actually *do* with a sunset as a Virgo, unless of course you're a painter or poet? Being, as opposed to doing, is not a concept you grasp readily. If something isn't useful, you've rarely much time for it and you'll simply push the mental 'delete' button.

Ordering Chaos

Your life runs on a dynamic tension between order and disorder and, until you find some way of understanding and categorising the chaotic broth of life, you can feel out of control and tossed about at the mercy of the unknown, something which terrifies you. You enjoy breaking things down into neat and manageable bite-sized pieces that will slot into your tidy mental model of the universe. Your mind is like one of those flow charts with arrows and lists, found in offices and laboratories, showing how everything interconnects and what their various functions are. (It was in fact a Virgo chemist, Sir Hans Krebs, who worked out the most important flow diagram for the breakdown of all foodstuffs.) Anything that you can't place on your mental map is beyond the pale and you prefer to ignore it and let it fade away into the background from whence it came.

To the Point

Accuracy, precision and meticulous attention to detail are all-important to you. Sweeping generalisations you can find irritating and downright offensive. Because you've a horror of being misinterpreted, you can easily become pedantic and go on and on about endless trivia long after your listeners' eyes have glazed over. There are some Virgos you daren't ask about their operation, work-in-progress or the film they've just seen – unless you're prepared for a blow-by-blow account, complete with commentary, that could easily last longer than the event itself.

Fine Tuning

Sifting and separating the essential from the trivial, the truth from the untruth and the authentic from the phoney is as instinctive to you as breathing. Your body, emotions, mind and intuition are delicate and finely tuned instruments. It is this acute sensitivity which makes your powers of discrimination so effective at pinpointing whether something is spot on or 'off message', but it comes at a price.

Everything around you, from emotional tension to sloppy eating habits and inaccuracy of detail, leaves its impression on you – much more so than you probably realise – so it's important that you avoid negativity as much as possible, especially your own home-grown variety.

Three in One

Virgo, Libra and Scorpio are said to have formed a single sign in the distant past. Once you decide to achieve or examine something, you'll combine Scorpio's intensity and determination to penetrate right to the very core and the Libran trait of scrupulously weighing up and evaluating every last detail to make sure that no facet has been overlooked, with the Virgoan quest for purity and precision. Sometimes Virgos drive themselves and others crazy, with their analysis-to-paralysis of themselves and everything else around them. But it is this talent for dissection and then synthesis, plus your adaptability, that allows you to shift into new situations and roles quickly, easily and utterly appropriately.

Realism and Compassion

It's hard to fool a Virgo. You are not naive and can see right through fakes and hypocrisy. It's part of your mission in life to find flaws to adjust and correct; giving helpful and constructive analyses is – potentially – one of your greatest gifts. However, it's only too easy for analysis to degenerate into carping and fault-finding and some Virgos are experts in the art of crushingly contemptuous criticism. Every sign can benefit from an injection of the better qualities of its opposite, which in your case is Pisces. Weaving some Piscean compassion and loving acceptance, both for yourself and others, into your way of operating will soften your sharpness and ease the sometimes intolerable burdens and expectations you have of yourself and others.

The Art of the Possible

Some Virgos, when faced with an unfamiliar challenge, freeze into immobility, unable to get started; they're scared to take the risk of getting things wrong and so do nothing at all. It may help to remember that when an aircraft flies towards its destination, it's off-course over 90 per cent of the time. A pilot's expertise lies in making constant small adjustments to keep the plane headed in the right direction. Improvising and adjusting to the needs of the moment are your particular skills and you learn best from hands-on experience and trial and error. So when you let yourself off the hook and drop the notion that you must always be right, even at the first attempt, and stop attempting to write the history of the world when a two-paragraph synopsis is all that's required, you actually become much more effective.

Less is More

Most Virgos, however, are far too realistic to believe that perfection can ever be achieved in this world of limitations. Your goal is to build the best possible bridge between the ideal and the possible without compromising the essence.

Your no-nonsense approach cuts through all that's redundant and goes right to the heart of the matter. A story about Michelangelo illustrates this point. One day Michelangelo went to the quarry and picked out a huge block of marble. The quarry master visited his studio many months later to see the marble transformed into an exquisite angel. He was astounded and asked Michelangelo how he'd managed it. Michelangelo replied simply that he'd just chipped away everything that wasn't angel. You, too, are a great chipper and stripper away of all that is superfluous to requirements for your desired result. Often at home too you'll feel more comfortable with a pared-down minimalist lifestyle and decor.

Waste and Efficiency

You have a sound commercial instinct and the ability to spot a good investment. Being well aware that time, energy and resources are limited, you can't bear to waste any of them. Some of your favourite phrases are 'Money Off' and 'Save £££s'. But in your drive for economy, you can stockpile caseloads of bargain items to save a few pence, and forget till later that you're actually not all that fond of pear and pilchard pâté or lilac loo rolls.

You're not necessarily a skinflint but you do like value for money and, unless you have a generous helping of fire in your chart, spontaneous splashing around of cash is just not your style. As Virgo Joseph P. Kennedy wrote to his son, the future American President John F. Kennedy: 'Dear Jack. Don't buy a single vote more than necessary. I'll be damned if I'm going to pay for a landslide.'

Improving Ways

Because you are not complacent or self-satisfied, you may undervalue your contribution and undercharge for your services. True humility, however, is a realistic assessment of your own worth. Once you've learned to overcome false modesty, you are perfectly capable of asking a fair rate for work well done. You get immense satisfaction from finding better and more efficient ways of doing things, but you've very little time for change for its own sake. If you have found a method that works, you are content to leave well alone. If it ain't broke, why fix it? You love trying to improve yourself too. Virgos must make up a sizeable proportion of the market for self-help books.

Practical Matters

Many Virgos are literal-minded and sceptical about anything which can't be demonstrated or shown to work. Practical solutions to problems interest you more than fancy theories. Virgos are the original doubting Thomases and you tend to question and challenge practically everything, wanting authoritative references, complete with detailed footnotes. You may be fascinated by the psychological and the mystical and can become a skilled practitioner once you find a system that categorises them properly – like astrology, graphology or numerology. Your humour tends to be clever, stylish and sharply witty and you love to play with quotations. Like Geminis, many Virgos are truly wicked mimics, summing up their victims mercilessly in a few telling gestures.

You are ultra-touchy about any suggestion that you have been incompetent or haven't done a job properly. With your constant self-criticism, you don't need any outside help, thank you very much. When angry, you are likely to become cantankerous, irritable, shrewish and sulky. You can then use your verbal and critical skills to fillet your opponent with quite devastating accuracy; but if you learn to deal with comments and differences of opinion as if they were intellectual discussions, you soon get over them.

At Your Service

Your identity and how you feel about yourself is bound up with your work. If your work is going well, you are well, and vice versa. The whole point of your life is to be of service – which has nothing at all to do with being subservient. A Virgo without a satisfying and meaningful occupation is a lost soul indeed. It doesn't matter what it is, as long as you can see some purpose in it. There is very little that gives you more pleasure and sense of pride than a job – big or small – skilfully completed. It must have been a Virgo who came up with the saying – 'What's worth doing is worth doing well.' You usually prefer to respond to an invitation or to circumstances, though, rather than start up some project by yourself, unless you've first established that there really is a call for what you provide. You'll rarely waste time on mere possibilities.

Doing it Your Way

Unless you are self-employed, where you can have all the important details under your control, you may prefer someone else to take overall responsibility. Many Virgos excel at working as second-in-command. Being accountable for inefficient folks below you is your quickest route to an ulcer or a nervous breakdown. You like to be left alone to work in your own way and can't stand anyone interfering, rushing you or messing with your schedules. Titles and honours don't particularly motivate you, but you do like appreciation, or at the very least acknowledgement, for a job well done.

You enjoy jobs with some kind of concrete result to show at the end of them. Once you've learned the ropes, you are excellent at improvising, as you are at your ingenious best taking ideas and material from many different sources and transforming and polishing them into something better and more effective. Being neat, methodical and conscientious, careers requiring skill and precision are right up your street.

Crafting a Career

Anything to do with healthcare could be an excellent choice, in either the orthodox or alternative fields. As you love finding out how things work, and delight in improving efficiency, psychology or engineering could also be attractive. Many fine artists, writers, actors and craftsmen are Virgos. Their keynote is often their versatility and increasing professionalism as the years go by. You could also find a niche in publishing, finance or business but, unless the element of fire is writ large in your chart, entrepreneurial risk-taking is not your style and you'll prefer to hedge your bets to keep your assets well protected.

Virgo and Health

Virgo is the natural sign of healing, as it is associated with the mind–body connection. Although, like the other mutable signs, Gemini, Sagittarius and Pisces, you can be prone to frequent minor ailments caused by temporary depletion of energy, when you take time out to rest you usually bounce back quickly. If you're typical of your sign, you'll look after yourself well, laying an excellent foundation for long-term health – and you'll probably age well and look younger than your years.

Conservative Virgos tend to prefer conventional medicine and their bathroom cupboards are like scaled-down pharmacies, with every common ailment from piles to pimples fully catered for. Alternative types prefer more natural methods. One I know, even when travelling, grew fresh greenery in a jar, which dangled neatly off the end of his rucksack. It's best not to take food fads and germ warfare too far, though. Cleanliness may be next to godliness, but your body usually prefers the middle way.

Virgo rules the liver and small intestines. Nervous tension can play havoc with your digestion and too much stress can lead to exhaustion and burn-out. Your body, like your mind, is acutely sensitive so you need to be discriminating about what you put into both. Pure food, air and water, and protecting yourself from anything negative – emotions, thoughts or grumbling acquaintances – especially before eating or sleeping is your best health insurance.

Space and Togetherness

Like many Virgos, you may find that, by choice or circumstance, you live alone for a period of time, learning to become self-contained, while deepening your relationship with yourself. It's often only then that you're able to open up to love and take a partner without risking dependency or compromising either your work or integrity. Any partner must respect your work and preferably take an active interest in it. In relationships, you may be torn between the powerful appeal of solitude and your desire for intimacy; it's important to negotiate the right ratio for you and your partner between time alone and togetherness, as both are essential for your well-being.

Hearts and Minds

Some Virgos have many relationships over the years but never fully commit to one, because what they're looking for is an authentic meeting of mind, body and spirit, with an equal, and nothing else will do. They would rather be alone than compromise. Others are less demanding and are realistic enough to accept that perfection is not an option on this planet. Once you've made up your mind about who you want to be with, commitment and monogamy come easily and, unless major problems develop, you'll stay devoted. However, if a relationship does die, despite every possible remedy being applied to revive it, you are capable of cutting the bonds with the cool precision of a surgeon. You've no time for things that don't work and can't be mended. When it's over, it's over.

Neat and Tidy

Virgos aren't taken in by superficial appearances. If the mind doesn't match up to even the most perfect of bodywork, you'll rapidly lose interest; intelligent communication is a must for you. Crudeness, stupidity, carelessness and sentimentality, not to mention bad manners and lack of laundering, are major turn-offs too. Anyone who chooses you must be prepared for your endless rituals for creating order; all the black shoes having to go on one shelf and the blue ones on another, the agonising about whether this pair is just dark navy or really black. And a veil is best drawn over what happens when your partner's possessions wander out of their natural habitat into yours . . .

Fiery Passions

There is something about fire types that attracts you like a magnet – people with Aries, Leo and Sagittarius strong in their charts. Fire people are flamboyant, spontaneous and fun-loving risk-takers, quite the opposite of your caution and conscientiousness. They can help you loosen up and enjoy life while you can help them deal with practical matters. If both of you learn to respect and appreciate your differences, this can be a winning combination.

Sex and the Virgin

Some people make the mistake of confusing Virgoan love of purity with uptightness and prudery. Usually this assessment is well wide of the mark. Think of Freddie Mercury, Ursula Andress and Sean Connery, sex symbols one and all, and who wrote the sizzlers *Lady Chatterley's Lover* and *Peyton Place* but Virgos D.H. Lawrence and Grace Metalious.

Although Virgos, when so inclined, can manage to live without sex better than almost any other sign apart from Pisces, most are not so inclined. Being an earth sign, you can be sensuous and passionate when aroused, but it may take time to warm you up. Some Virgos like to schedule sex so that it slots in neatly between their work activities. Check out their appointment books and you might find a discreet little 's' with a neat circle round it entered for certain times.

Before you can relax and let your hair down, you like to get all the little details attended to first. One Virgo I know enjoys a bit of a frolic on the kitchen table because the bin is nice and handy to dispose of love's leftovers. Partners who are less than meticulously attentive to personal hygiene have zero chance of snuggling up between your lavender-scented sheets. When you finally get round to it, your sensitivity and delicacy allow you to be aware of your partner's needs and if you feel valued you are, in the bedroom, what you are in the rest of life – skilful.

SIX

Aspects of the Sun

PLANETS, JUST LIKE PEOPLE, CAN HAVE IMPORTANT RELATIONSHIPS with each other. These relationships are called aspects. Aspects to your Sun from any other planet can influence your personality markedly. The most powerful effects come with those from the slower-moving planets – Saturn, Uranus, Neptune or Pluto. Sometimes they can alter your ideas about yourself and your behaviour patterns so much that you may not feel at all typical of your sign in certain areas of your life.

Check if your birth date and year appear in the various sections below to find out if one or more of these planets was aspecting the Sun when you were born. Only the so-called challenging aspects have been included. These are formed when the planets are together, opposite or at right angles to each other in the sky.

Unfortunately, because space is restricted, other aspects have been left out, although they have similar effects to those described below and, for the same reason, a few dates will inevitably have been missed out, too. (You can find out for sure whether or not your Sun is aspected at my website

www.janeridderpatrick.com) If your Sun has no aspects to
Saturn, Uranus, Neptune or Pluto, you're more likely to be
a typical Virgo.

Some well-known Virgos with challenging aspects to
their Suns appear below. You can find more in the birthday
section at the end of the book.

Sun in Virgo in Aspect with Saturn
If you were born between 1948 and 1950, or 1978 and 1980,
whether or not your birthday is listed below, you are likely
to feel the influence of Saturn on your Sun.

23 August–2 September in: 1935, 1941–2, 1949, 1957, 1964–5,
1971, 1978, 1986 and 1994
3–12 September in: 1936, 1942, 1949–50, 1957–8, 1965, 1972–3,
1979, 1987, 1994
13–23 September in: 1936, 1943, 1950–51, 1958–9, 1966, 1972–3,
1980, 1988, 1995

Martin Amis	Jonathan Aitken	Stephen Fry
Claudia Schiffer	Clara Schumann	Raine Spencer

You have a powerful ambition to gain some kind of official
acknowledgement that you are a person of substance and
worth. This could motivate you to work hard until you are
part of the establishment yourself. Your secret dread of
being found inadequate, in either your efficiency, education
or communication skills, may, however, tempt you to hold
back from even trying for fear you'll be disapproved of, or
shamed in some way.

You can't bear criticism and this aspect makes you ultra-
sensitive to just that. Your father may have been a
disappointing, or disappointed, man or could have made
heavy demands on you – the kind of person who, when you

came home from school with four A grades and a B, would ask what went wrong that you didn't get five As. If you were harshly treated in childhood, you may tend to be hard on others too. Stepping out of this cycle can be one of the greatest gifts that you can give yourself. So can learning to develop compassion for yourself, and others, and to keep your disparaging attitude – and tongue – in good check.

You'll never find peace from your potentially crippling dips in self-confidence or acquire a real sense of achievement until you stop looking for outside approval. Taking shortcuts to success won't work, as you'll almost certainly be caught; prominent politician Jonathan Aitken ended up in prison for perjury. By setting your own standards for success and service, then working towards them patiently and responsibly, you can create and express the you that will live up to your own high expectations. When you bite the bullet and do this, turning stumbling blocks into stepping stones, you can achieve lasting respect, success and recognition in your field for work well done.

Sun in Virgo in Aspect with Uranus
If you were born between 1962 and 1968, whether or not your birthday is listed below, you are likely to feel the influence of Uranus on your Sun.

23 August–2 September in: 1941–4, 1961–5 and 1982–5
3–12 September in: 1943–7, 1964–7 and 1986–7
13–23 September in: 1944–8, 1966–9 and 1987–9

Kate Adie	Freddie Mercury	Grandma Moses
Mary Shelley	Twiggy	H.G. Wells

You dare to be different. Uranus, planet of reform, shock and progress, urges you to challenge and change the way things are. Grandma Moses took up painting in 1939 at the age of 75 and went on to enjoy phenomenal success; stick-thin model Twiggy changed the shape of fashion for years to come; Kate Adie was one of the first woman war correspondents, previously a strictly male-only territory; and Mary Shelley was prophetically ahead of her time with her book *Frankenstein* about a man-made monster who turned destructive because he felt so terribly isolated. You too may know the loneliness of being out on a limb, but also its excitement. At best, you have a crystal-clear view of what is outdated or unfair in a system and have stimulating and often controversial ideas of how to bring about improvements. At worst, you can be a bit of an oddball or downright contrary. You may have an attitude problem around tradition and authority, which, of course, could provoke the almost inevitable backlash. Chances are, though, that many of your ideas that seem weird today will be mainstream a few years down the line.

Because you love working on new and exciting projects, when the novelty wears off and a job becomes humdrum or too successful you'll tend to get restless. Be careful not to sabotage your own good work by throwing it away and moving on too abruptly just for the sake of a change. Your father may have been unusual, or remote, in some way and if you are a woman a conventional marriage or home situation may prove difficult. An arrangement that allows you space and freedom may be much more to your liking.

Sun in Virgo in Aspect with Neptune
If you were born between 1929 and 1942, whether or not your birthday is listed below, you are likely to feel the influence of Neptune on your Sun.

23 August–2 September in: 1928–33 or 1970–76
3–12 September in: 1933–8 and 1974–81
13–23 September in: 1938–43 or 1979–86

| Lady Antonia Fraser | Sean Connery | Patsy Cline |
| Ludwig II of Bavaria | Man Ray | Jean Rhys |

Neptune allows you to tap into the world of fantasies, yearnings and dreams – your own and other people's – and to express them in some way. Ludwig II of Bavaria, known as the fairy-tale king, built many exquisitely grandiose castles, including Neuschwanstein, the inspiration for Disney's Cinderella castle. Things are rarely quite what they seem when Neptune is involved. The photographer Man Ray was a master of illusion and glamour. One of his most famous photographs is of tears on a woman's face, which were actually glycerine, but the image caught a haunting note of poignancy. Others may see you, or your husband or father, as a victim, a saviour or some kind of icon. You may have idealised your father or found that he was emotionally unavailable for you in some way, either because he wasn't around, was too busy helping others, or had escaped into an addiction. Lady Antonia Fraser's father, Lord Longford, was a committed Christian and socialist who devoted much of his later life to prison reform.

You may have vague feelings of helplessness and unworthiness. Writer Jean Rhys once described herself as a doormat in a world of boots. (Pluto also aspected her Sun.) Alternatively, you could be the one looking after life's lame ducks and victims. It can be hard for you to say 'no' and you could take on too much because you feel guilty and responsible for righting the woes of the world. Your salvation comes through finding an ideal to serve and pouring your whole heart into it. You've a need to check out regularly from everyday reality. It's best, though, if your escapism doesn't involve alcohol or food; poetry, films or music, or even just daydreaming, are much more wholesome soul food.

Sun in Virgo in Aspect with Pluto

If you were born between 1957 and 1971, whether or not your birthday is listed below, you are likely to feel the influence of Pluto on your Sun.

23 August–2 September in: 1955–63 and 1995–2000
3–12 September in: 1961–8
13–23 September in: 1966–73

| Francis Chichester | Greta Garbo | William Golding |
| Michael Jackson | Joseph P. Kennedy | Beverly Nichols |

The use or abuse of power is likely to touch your life in one way or another. Beverly Nichols, an American writer known for his charming pieces on gardening and cats, revealed a darker, hidden side of his childhood in his book *Father Figure*, telling of his sadistic, alcoholic father, whom Nichols tried to murder three times.

Some with this aspect refuse to tolerate corruption, hypocrisy or bullying and will not rest until they've exposed the culprits and rooted them out. Others can be a bit dictatorial themselves. You have the determination and skill to go against the odds and into extreme conditions or taboo territory to achieve success. Despite brushes with death, injuries and suffering from lung cancer, Francis Chichester made successful solo transatlantic and round-the-world yacht trips between the ages of 65 and 67. Your bid for power could also be financial. Joseph Kennedy, founder of the American Kennedy clan, made a fortune in the depression when others were going broke, to advance his political ambitions through his sons. Do be careful, though, not to be too pushy and so, inadvertently, put people's backs up. You may find yourself in relationships involving power struggles, some of them provoked or made worse by your fear, vulnerability or unwillingness to compromise. Peace comes when you stop trying to control the world and learn to trust life.

You may have a sense of having something unacceptable about you which you constantly try to change or eliminate, sometimes through psychotherapy or even with surgery. Multimillionaire singer Michael Jackson has radically altered his appearance over the years. You probably sense that you'll have to leave the past behind and reinvent yourself at some time. This should be a cause for celebration, not for barricading yourself in against change.

SEVEN

Meeting Your Moon

☽ THE GLYPH FOR THE MOON IS THE SEMI-CIRCLE OR CRESCENT. It is a symbol for the receptiveness of the soul and is associated with feminine energies and the ebb and flow of the rhythms of life. In some Islamic traditions it represents the gateway to paradise and the realms of bliss.

The Sun and Moon are the two complementary poles of your personality, like yang and yin, masculine and feminine, active and reflective, career and home, father and mother. The Moon comes into its own as a guide at night, the time of sleeping consciousness. It also has a powerful effect on the waters of the earth. Likewise, the Moon in your birth chart describes what you respond to instinctively and feel 'in your waters', often just below the level of consciousness. It is your private radar system, sending you messages via your body responses and feelings, telling you whether a situation seems safe or scary, nice or nasty. Feelings provide vital information about circumstances in and around you. Ignore them at your peril; that will lead you into emotional, and sometimes even physical, danger. Eating disorders tend to be associated with being out of touch with, or neglecting, the instincts and the body, both of which the Moon describes.

Extraordinary though it might seem to those who are emotionally tuned in, some people have great difficulty in knowing what they are feeling. One simple way is to pay attention to your body. Notice any sensations that attract your attention. Those are linked to your feelings. Now get a sense of whether they are pleasant or unpleasant, then try to put a more exact name to what those feelings might be. Is it sadness, happiness, fear? What is it that they are trying to tell you? Your Moon hints at what will strongly activate your feelings. Learning to trust and decode this information will help make the world seem – and be – a safer place.

The Moon represents your drive to nurture and protect yourself and others. Its sign, house and aspects describe how you respond and adapt emotionally to situations and what feeds you, in every sense of the word. It gives information about your home and home life and how you experienced your mother, family and childhood, as well as describing your comfort zone of what feels familiar – the words 'family' and 'familiar' come from the same source. It shows, too, what makes you feel secure and what could comfort you when you're feeling anxious. Your Moon describes what moves and motivates you powerfully at the deepest instinctual level and indicates what is truly the 'matter' in – or with – your life.

Knowing children's Moon signs can help parents and teachers better understand their insecurities and respect their emotional make-up and needs, and so prevent unnecessary hurt, or even harm, to sensitive young lives. It's all too easy to expect that our children and parents should have the same emotional wiring as we do, but that's rarely how life works. Finding our parents' Moon signs can be a real revelation. It can often help us understand where they are coming from, what they need and why they react to us in the way they do. Many of my clients have been able to find the understanding and compassion to forgive their parents when they realised that they were doing their very best with the emotional resources available to them.

In relationships it is important that your Moon's requirements are met to a good enough extent. For example, if you have your Moon in Sagittarius you must have adventure, freedom and the opportunity to express your beliefs. If being with your partner constantly violates these basic needs, you will never feel secure and loved and the relationship could, in the long term, undermine you. However, if your Moon feels too comfortable, you will never change and grow. The art is to get a good working balance between support and challenge.

A man's Moon sign can show some of the qualities he will unconsciously select in a wife or partner. Some of the others are shown in his Venus sign. Many women can seem much more like their Moon signs than their Sun signs, especially if they are involved in mothering a family and being a support system for their husbands or partners. It is only at the mid-life crisis that many women start to identify more with the qualities of their own Suns rather than living that out through their partners' ambitions. Similarly, men tend to live out the characteristics of their Moon signs through their wives and partners until mid-life, often quite cut off from their own feelings and emotional responses. If a man doesn't seem at all like his Moon sign, then check out the women in his life. There's a good chance that his wife, mother or daughter will show these qualities.

Your Moon can be in any sign, including the same one as your Sun. Each sign belongs to one of the four elements: Fire, Earth, Air or Water. The element of your Moon can give you a general idea of how you respond to new situations and what you need to feel safe and comforted. We all become anxious if our Moon's needs are not being recognised and attended to. We then, automatically, go into our personal little rituals for making ourselves feel better. Whenever you are feeling distressed, especially when you are way out of your comfort zone in an unfamiliar situation, do something to feed and soothe your Moon. You're almost certain to calm down quickly.

Fire Moons

If you have a fire Moon in Aries, Leo or Sagittarius, your first response to any situation is to investigate in your imagination the possibilities for drama, excitement and self-expression. Feeling trapped by dreary routine in an ordinary humdrum life crushes you completely. Knowing that you are carrying out a special mission feeds your soul. To you, all the world's a stage and a voyage of discovery. Unless you are at the centre of the action playing some meaningful role, anxiety and depression can set in. To feel secure, you have to have an appropriate outlet for expressing your spontaneity, honourable instincts and passionate need to be of unique significance. The acknowledgement, appreciation and feedback of people around you are essential, or you don't feel real. Not to be seen and appreciated, or to be overlooked, can feel like a threat to your very existence.

Earth Moons

If you have an earth Moon in Taurus, Virgo or Capricorn, you'll respond to new situations cautiously and practically. Rapidly changing circumstances where you feel swept along and out of control are hard for you to cope with. You need time for impressions to sink in. Sometimes it is only much later, after an event has taken place, that you become sure what you felt about it. Your security lies in slowing down, following familiar routines and rituals, even if they are a bit obsessive, and focusing on something, preferably material – possibly the body itself or nature – which is comforting because it is still there. Indulging the senses in some way often helps too, through food, sex or body care. So does taking charge of the practicalities of the immediate situation, even if this is only mixing the drinks or passing out clipboards. To feel secure, you need continuity and a sense that you have your hand on the rudder of your own life. Think of the rather irreverent joke about the man seeming to cross himself in a crisis, all the while actually touching his most valued possessions to check that they are still intact – spectacles, testicles, wallet and watch. That must have been thought up by someone with the Moon in an earth sign.

Air Moons

When your Moon is in an air sign – Gemini, Libra or Aquarius – you feel most secure when you can stand back from situations and observe them from a distance. Too much intimacy chokes you and you'll tend to escape it by going into your head to the safety of ideas and analysis. Even in close relationships you need your mental, and preferably physical, space. You often have to think, talk or write about what you are feeling before you are sure what your feelings are. By putting them 'out there' so that you can examine them clearly, you can claim them as your own. Unfairness and unethical behaviour can upset you badly and make you feel uneasy until you have done something about it or responded in some way. It can be easy with an air Moon to be unaware of, or to ignore, your own feelings because you are more responsive to ideas, people and situations outside of yourself that may seem to have little connection with you. This is not a good idea, as it cuts you off from the needs of your body as well as your own emotional intelligence. Making opportunities to talk, play with and exchange ideas and information can reduce the stress levels if anxiety strikes.

Water Moons

Finally, if your Moon is in a water sign – Cancer, Scorpio or Pisces – you are ultra-sensitive to atmospheres, and you can experience other people's pain or distress as if they were your own. You tend to take everything personally and, even if the situation has nothing at all to do with you, feel responsible for making it better. Your worst nightmare is to feel no emotional response coming back from other people. That activates your deep-seated terror of abandonment, which can make you feel that you don't exist and is, quite literally, what you fear even more than death. If you feel insecure, you may be tempted to resort to emotional manipulation to try to force intimacy with others – not a good idea, as this can lead to the very rejection that you dread. You are at your most secure when the emotional climate is positive and you have trusted, supportive folk around who will winkle you out of hiding if you become too reclusive. With a water Moon, it is vital to learn to value your own feelings and to take them seriously – and to have a safe, private place you can retreat to when you feel emotionally fragile. As you never forget anything which has made a feeling impression on you, sometimes your reactions are triggered by unconscious memories of things long past, rather than what is taking place in the present. When you learn to interpret them correctly, your feelings are your finest ally and will serve you well.

Finding Your Moon Sign

If you don't yet know your Moon sign, before looking it up, you could have some fun reading through the descriptions that follow and seeing if you can guess which one it is. To find your Moon sign, check your year and date of birth in the tables on pp. 99–112. For a greater in-depth understanding of your Moon sign, you might like to read about its characteristics in the book in this series about that sign.

At the beginning of each section are the names of some well-known Virgos with that particular Moon sign. You can find more about them in Chapter Ten.

Sun in Virgo with Moon in Aries

Richard Attenborough	Lauren Bacall	Ingrid Bergman
Roald Dahl	Jeremy Irons	Alexander McCall Smith

Sinking your teeth into a fresh challenge puts a spring in your step and a song in your heart. Your best work is often done when you're having to compete. It doesn't matter whether this is against the clock, a rival, or your own previous achievements. Action or aggression is likely to play a major role in your life somewhere. Roald Dahl wrote some of the best-loved children's stories ever, but many teachers and parents object to them because of the violence and anarchy they contain. You're unlikely to be one of life's bystanders, as you are at your most comfortable when you're actively involved in whatever situation you find yourself in. Roald Dahl, again, once saw police beating up a black youth in London and instead of driving past, as most people would, he actively intervened, then got the press involved.

With so much energy at your disposal, you can whip through your tasks at lightning speed. The author Alexander McCall Smith turns out a couple of thousand beautifully crafted words before breakfast and going on to his high-calibre day job. You're rarely scared to take a risk, and not being overly burdened by the self-doubt and inhibitions that hold other Virgos back, you'll often do your own thing no matter what anyone thinks, or whatever the consequences. Ingrid Bergman ran off with a married man, leaving her husband and child, at a time when, even for Hollywood, that was utterly scandalous and suffered torrents of abuse because of it. Depending whether you use your energy selflessly or selfishly, you can be a force for creativity or destruction, for yourself as well as others. Obviously, then, choosing wisely matters.

Sun in Virgo with Moon in Taurus

Laura Ashley	Queen Elizabeth I	Greta Garbo
Hugh Grant	Prince Harry	Mother Teresa

Your down-to-earth approach to whatever life throws at you makes you a tower of strength through good times or bad. Like a still pool of peace, your presence is calming and reassuring and you can be relied upon to provide practical help and guidance. Mother Teresa devoted her life to the sick and poor of the slums of Calcutta dealing, lovingly and unruffled, with the needs of each moment.

Abrupt changes are hard for you to handle. Anything that you can't predict or control, or that moves too fast, can unsettle you, making you feel insecure, so you may try to ignore or ridicule it away or resort to stubborn, arms-folded resistance. Your need for on-going stability can make you a bit of a control freak, and often a good politician. Queen Elizabeth I set up an elaborate and meticulously recorded spy system to make sure she kept her finger on the pulse of current affairs. Probably the worst way to torment you is to move everything on your mantelpiece just half an inch away from its normal position.

You need to process new emotional information, a bit like a cow chewing over the cud. It's not that you can't handle change; you just need time – and plenty of it – to make adjustments. When feeling anxious, you may resort automatically to sensual pleasures. Hugh Grant eventually revealed that the embarrassing episode when he was caught in the act with a hooker was the result of the stress of feeling he'd messed up a role. No excuse, of course, for bad behaviour but it's an explanation that Moon in Taurus people will easily understand. Peace and tranquillity and being left alone to potter are important to help you unwind.

Sun in Virgo with Moon in Gemini

John Buchan	Shirley Conran	Buddy Holly
Ludwig II of Bavaria	Grandma Moses	Claudia Schiffer

Your Gemini Moon picks up instinctively what is currently 'in the air' and about to become a trend – and you'll want to pass the information on. Virgo needs to be of service and to do or make something useful with whatever material comes your way. Combining the two allows you to tune in to the demands of the moment and notice what needs doing right under your nose – then get on and do it, efficiently.

You can't bear to be tied down to too much routine. With your low boredom threshold, a career that offers plenty of short-term and varied tasks, where you have to come up with ingenious and practical solutions, especially with limited resources, is right up your street. You may even prefer to have two or more jobs, or homes, to hop, skip and jump between. As well as being a prolific and gifted writer, John Buchan, author of *The Thirty-Nine Steps*, was also a highly regarded statesman, historian and Governor General of Canada.

At home you're likely to have the radio, television and computer on at the same time, and still manage to sneak a look at the newspapers. Being a born communicator, you're at your most comfortable when you are talking or writing about what you feel or think. You make an excellent reporter, commentator, writer and mimic, as you are quick to pick up the essence of what is going on and, with a few deft words, gestures or strokes of the pen, pass it on to others, helping them feel they are experiencing what you are. With your quiet charm and wit, and way with words, you're unlikely to find much difficulty in coaxing others to fall in with your plans.

Sun in Virgo with Moon in Cancer

Lady Antonia Fraser	Jessica Mitford	Van Morrison
Keanu Reaves	Clara Schumann	Upton Sinclair

Being naturally timid and self-protective, as well as afraid of being wrong or inappropriate, you need gentle encouragement, clear instructions and a great deal of reassurance to help you move out of your safe and familiar habits and habitat. If your childhood was harsh and rejecting, to keep yourself safe, you are likely to have built up formidable emotional defences against feeling too much. This, sadly, can cut you off from the intimacy you need if you're to flourish. You may also be prone to irrational fears and phobias, but the good news is that you can quickly learn strategies for overcoming your anxiety and feeling safe in the world.

Being highly intuitive, you can pick up on atmospheres instantly, tune in to the feelings of those around you and establish excellent rapport. You are quick to go to the defence of those in need and can find it unbearable if others are being hurt or humiliated. Jessica Mitford was inspired to write her exposé, *The American Way of Death*, when she found out about the excessive funeral costs for her lawyer husband's poor clients. You feel deeply and are easily moved to tears, something that you may try to suppress, as you may feel ashamed of feeling so out of control.

Your family, chosen or biological, matters a great deal to you and, regardless of your gender, you have a powerful instinct to mother – though this may be creative projects as often as children. You need to feel mothered yourself, and tune in to the natural rhythms of the day and year. So treat yourself kindly, plump up the pillows and curl up in bed with a hot, comforting drink as soon as the sun goes down.

Sun in Virgo with Moon in Leo

Cherie Blair	Stephen Fry	King Louis XIV of France
Elsa Schiaparelli	Twiggy	Dinah Washington

Behind your modest exterior there's a creative artist – and exhibitionist – just waiting to break out. Sometimes it manages, as in the case of designer Elsa Schiaparelli, whose sensational styles and stunning colours just knocked the socks off the fashion-conscious from the 1930s onwards. Her signature was 'shocking pink'. Like her, nothing you do is likely to go unnoticed – not if you have anything to do with it anyway. Being overlooked or feeling insignificant can make you anxious so it's vital that you find an honourable role to play, where it is appropriate to stand in the spotlight, radiating generosity, leadership, service and integrity. More than likely, you're a natural leader, with formidable organising skills. Louis XIV, known as the Sun King, made all the important state decisions himself ('L'état, c'est moi' – I *am* the state) and under his patronage, throughout the longest reign in European history, the arts flourished with brilliance.

As you hate to see yourself presented in a bad light, you'll tend to act honourably in any position of responsibility. If your dignity is ruffled, though, or your work is criticised, offenders had better duck for cover to avoid your regal 'off with his head' displeasure. With your big-hearted generosity, natural charisma and majestic bearing, you've a knack of getting your own way, and that is exactly how you like it.

Playing with children can help bring out the spontaneous child in you, and allow you to drop, for a while at least, your workaholic tendencies. Sometimes a Leo Moon indicates that you come from a prominent family or that you have a powerful, dramatic or even domineering mother. It certainly means that you are at your best in a home you can be proud of.

Sun in Virgo with Moon in Virgo

| Martin Amis | Sean Connery | Frederick Forsyth |
| Derek Nimmo | Graham Sutherland | William Wilberforce |

Nothing is likely to pass your scrutiny. Your most stringent and critical attention is often turned on yourself, usually to positive effect. A case in point is actor Sean Connery, whose total professionalism and technical expertise are legendary in a business famous for its prima donnas. He learns quickly and he's always on time, in place and word-perfect. Some with this combination are highly strung and irritable and can be carping critics or fusspots when things aren't running smoothly.

You've a sharp eye for flaws and you may have to learn to focus more on the beauty, wonders and minor miracles that surround you, rather than always on what's faulty, or you could become cynical or lost in endless to-do list-making. Problem-solving is your particular gift. You like to know how things work and be able to operate them yourself; this can be anything from social niceties, or systems of thinking, to mechanical contraptions, but whatever your interests you're likely to end up an expert, as you like to do things properly. Frederick Forsyth's thrillers, like *The Day of the Jackal*, *The Odessa File* and *The Dogs of War*, are all meticulously researched and precisely plotted.

Orderly rituals, even simple ones like sharpening your pencils or squeezing exactly the right amount of toothpaste onto your toothbrush, can be immensely comforting in times of stress. Finding work that you see as useful, of service or leading to some clearly defined end result, helps keep you grounded and brings out your finest qualities. William Wilberforce gave 19 years of his life and energy to putting an end to the slave trade in Britain and was only stopped by ill health from carrying on with the gruelling work of ending slavery all over the world.

Sun in Virgo with Moon in Libra

Agatha Christie   Pauline Collins   D.H. Lawrence
Kenneth More   Alan Pinkerton   Edgar Rice Burroughs

Making decisions can be tough, so you may do the rounds asking everyone else's opinion. While testing the water is important, if you don't bite the bullet and make a choice you'll be left feeling anxious and uncertain. Two things could hold you back. One is the twin Virgo bugbear: the fear of doing something inappropriate coupled with the unrealistic expectation that you should get it right first time round. The other is the Libran fear of being disliked. To say yes to one person or option is to say no to another, and as you hate to risk offending, you may hesitate too long and miss the moment. Let yourself off the hook; every single decision has to be made on insufficient evidence and you, of all people, are perfectly capable of making the necessary adjustments to the hitches that inevitably turn up in the best-laid of plans.

You can't bear ugliness, either of spirit or surroundings. Injustice riles you too and you may become actively involved in working to right what's wrong. You could focus so much on others that you neglect your own needs, then the balance will tip, leaving you sulking about how unfair life is to you. Your charm and ability to see everyone's point of view makes you a natural people person; just make sure you don't become a people-pleaser to keep the peace. It can also make you a formidable strategist, able to work out how others will act. Alan Pinkerton, founder of the American detective agency that bears his name, successfully foiled an assassination attempt on Abraham Lincoln on the way to his inauguration. He was also a campaigner for political rights for the working classes.

Sun in Virgo with Moon in Scorpio

| Prince Albert | Martin Bell | Bruno Bettelheim |
| A.S. Byatt | Maria Montessori | Raquel Welch |

You tend to be secretive about your innermost thoughts and feelings. People with this combination often radiate charisma and a subtle, smouldering sexuality. It would be surprising if life hadn't brought you into contact with sex, death, secrets or power, in one way or another, in early life, and it's possible that these themes could continue to fascinate or follow you into adult life. Bruno Bettelheim was a psychologist who investigated fairy tales and came to the conclusion that their often violent and brutal themes help children to deal with the darker aspects of their own lives in a safe way.

You have access to immense emotional power, which you can turn to making money, influencing political decisions in your own home patch and exposing and eliminating corruption. Your antennae are on constant alert to monitor threats to your survival, power, wealth or position, and you can spot when something is 'off' instantly, and will often feel compelled to step in to do something about it. Martin Bell, a BBC foreign correspondent known as 'the man in the white suit' because of the way he usually dressed, stood for parliament as an anti-sleaze candidate – and won – to prevent an opponent, whom he saw as deeply corrupt, getting in. When your back is against the wall, you may surprise even yourself with the survival resources you have at your disposal. You may seem meek and mild, but once you've set your heart on a goal, almost nothing will stop you. Maria Montessori, Italy's first woman doctor, developed her remarkable teaching method with children with learning difficulties in the slums of Rome. A mother herself, she never married and, despite the moral climate of the time, went on to establish a formidable international reputation.

Sun in Virgo with Moon in Sagittarius

Stephen King   Arthur Koestler   Freddie Mercury
Harry Secombe   Mary Shelley   Margaret Trudeau

Freddie Mercury's song 'I Want to Break Free' could easily be your theme tune. You are a free spirit and being tied down either to one place or to too many responsibilities can drive you crazy. It's not that you can't settle down, but fidelity may not come easily unless you find a partner who understands your need for adventure and informality and can share your enthusiasms and beliefs. Margaret Trudeau, wife of Canada's Prime Minister, couldn't stand the red tape and left the marriage to follow a hippy lifestyle; and Mary Shelley, writer of *Frankenstein*, eloped to Italy with the poet Percy Bysshe Shelley. Both left scandal in their wake. You may not go to such extremes but you've the soul of a gypsy and a wanderlust just beneath your surface that itches to be activated.

Underneath all the fun and love of being the sparkling entertainer is a part you'll rarely allow others to see – the lurking black dog of depression that can overwhelm you when you're alone and your faith deserts you. Yet you're usually able to bounce back and see the opportunities and the bright side of every situation, no matter how dire, as you're an eternal optimist. Harry Secombe, the singer and comedian, will always be remembered for his great good nature and a laugh that came right from the belly.

You've a powerful need to understand the meaning of life. This makes you a natural philosopher and you can see significance in even the small things that happen to you and to others. The combination of Virgo's attention to detail and Sagittarius's bursting need to teach can make you an excellent writer, broadcaster and adviser, well able to get your message across loud and clear.

Sun in Virgo with Moon in Capricorn

Patsy Cline	Lady Elizabeth	Dorothy Parker
	Longford	
Siegfried Sassoon	Neale Donald Walsch	Jimmy Young

Hard work, and sometimes hardship, is as familiar to you as breathing. Many with this combination have come from poor or humble backgrounds and work their way steadily to the top, or were raised in homes where correct behaviour and strict discipline were the rule, rather than spontaneity and warm acceptance. There's a bonus to early difficulties: you are well able to look after yourself. Unless you give in to the periodic depression that can dog you and just give up, you can put your all into achieving your ambitions, working hard and patiently to acquire the status, power and respect you crave. You may find it hard to stop though. Popular DJ Jimmy Young gave his last broadcast at the age of 81 and still felt he was retired too soon. You'll often feel more secure with some recognised credentials behind you. Working in a big organisation often has an appeal, and this can sometimes become like a substitute parent.

Brushes with life's problems will have made you realistic or even a little cynical and your ironic humour may cover up a deep layer of sadness. Dorothy Parker was known for her acid and often self-deprecating wit. You're prone to hiding emotional needs for fear of disapproval and have very little time for whingers and victims. In fact, you may not be averse to giving them a sharp verbal lashing to wake them up to reality. Oddly, solitude and sinking into melancholy feed you, so allow yourself to indulge in them occasionally, as well as taking time off to enjoy the fruits of your considerable labours too.

Sun in Virgo with Moon in Aquarius

Kate Adie	Edward Burne-Jones	Gustav Holst
Sophia Loren	Jessye Norman	H.G. Wells

Being a detached observer, messy emotions can disturb you, your own as well as other people's, and you'll sidestep them wherever possible. Unfortunately this can mean you ignore your body's messages about when it needs to be fed, watered and rested. Your moods can be quite contrary; others may feel you are aloof and even rather eccentric. Loyal friendships suit you better than wall-to-wall intimacy and if anybody tries to get too close, physically or emotionally, you'll start to feel jittery and trapped. Working with groups of like-minded people gives you great satisfaction, especially in humanitarian or ethical causes that aim to improve the human condition, like science and technology or social reform. As you look more to the future, tradition for its own sake irritates you and you'll rebel against conventions you feel are stupid or oppressive. H.G. Wells campaigned for free love, world government and human rights, as well as being a science fiction pioneer with such titles as *The First Men in the Moon* – published in 1900.

Your home is probably unusual or unconventional in some way and this suits you better than a tigh-knit, cosy, so-called normal nuclear family. Even if you have lived in the same house all your life, you may feel as though you are just camping, edgily waiting for the call to move on. This can stop you putting down emotional roots anywhere and may even lead to relationship tensions. Deep down, you feel the whole world is your family, and for contentment you need to find some way of widening your family home or circle to let the world in. Time on your own, as well as with friends, is essential for recharging your batteries.

Sun in Virgo with Moon in Pisces

Leonard Cohen	Macaulay Culkin	Johann von Goethe
Lenny Henry	James Hilton	Michael Jackson

James Hilton, in his novel *Lost Horizon*, describes the hidden valley of Shangri-La, a lost paradise on earth. You too long for a blissful retreat from this world of woes, and you may create it internally, floating through life as if in a dream. Michael Jackson created his literally. His home, Neverland, even has a private amusement park co-designed with Macaulay Culkin. You need frequent breaks from everyday reality, but be wary of seeking refuge in food or alcohol, as you can easily become addicted. Meditation, music, poetry or films are safer and saner options.

Suffering affects you powerfully because of your own fears of loss or abandonment and you are quick to reach out to help others. Being so acutely sensitive and imaginative, you can be badly affected, without even realising it, by negativity. You may have to struggle with issues of low self-esteem and victim-consciousness. At core, this is a deeply spiritual – as distinct from religious – combination, as you are aware that there is something more to life than your own small ego and that you are connected to whatever that is. For some, this is a scary notion, and they turn cynical as a defence against their own vulnerability. You've a knack of communicating, or acting out, what people yearn for, but which was unexpressed until you gave it form. Developing your natural intuitive gifts for some practical purpose can give you great satisfaction. Even more than other Virgos, you can feel dissatisfied until you've found an ideal to serve and dedicate your life to. Your dependency and fear of confrontation can tempt you to overlook or compromise your own needs in relationships – so steer well clear of selfish partners, often disguised as victims. You deserve the emotional support and encouragement you give readily to others, and need so much yourself.

EIGHT

Mercury – It's All in the Mind

THE GLYPHS FOR THE PLANETS ARE MADE UP OF THREE SYMBOLS: the circle, the semi-circle and the cross. Mercury is the only planet, apart from Pluto, whose glyph is made up of all three of these symbols. At the bottom there is the cross, representing the material world; at the top is the semi-circle of the crescent Moon, symbolising the personal soul; and in the middle, linking these two, is the circle of eternity, expressed through the individual. In mythology, Mercury was the only god who had access to all three worlds – the underworld, the middle world of earth and the higher world of the gods. Mercury in your chart represents your ability, through your thoughts and words, to make connections between the inner world of your mind and emotions, the outer world of other people and events, and the higher world of intuition. Your Mercury sign can give you a great deal of information about the way your mind works and about your interests, communication skills and your preferred learning style.

It can be frustrating when we just can't get through to some people and it's easy to dismiss them as being either completely thick or deliberately obstructive. Chances are they are neither. It may be that you're simply not talking each other's languages. Knowing your own and other people's communication styles can lead to major breakthroughs in relationships.

Information about children's natural learning patterns can help us teach them more effectively. It's impossible to learn properly if the material isn't presented in a way that resonates with the way your mind works. You just can't 'hear' it, pick it up or grasp it. Wires then get crossed and the data simply isn't processed. Many children are seriously disadvantaged if learning materials and environments don't speak to them. You may even have been a child like that yourself. If so, you could easily have been left with the false impression that you are a poor learner just because you couldn't get a handle on the lessons being taught. Identifying your own learning style can be like finding the hidden key to the treasure room of knowledge.

The signs of the zodiac are divided into four groups by element:

> The fire signs: Aries, Leo and Sagittarius
> The earth signs: Taurus, Virgo and Capricorn
> The air signs: Gemini, Libra and Aquarius
> The water signs: Cancer, Scorpio and Pisces

Your Mercury will therefore belong to one of the four elements, depending on which sign it is in. Your Mercury can only be in one of three signs – the same sign as your Sun, the one before or the one after. This means that each sign has one learning style that is never natural to it. For Virgo, this is the water style.

Mercury in each of the elements has a distinctive way of

operating. I've given the following names to the learning and communicating styles of Mercury through the elements. Mercury in fire – active imaginative; Mercury in earth – practical; Mercury in air – logical; and Mercury in water – impressionable.

Mercury in Fire: Active Imaginative

Your mind is wide open to the excitement of fresh ideas. It responds to action and to the creative possibilities of new situations. Drama, games and storytelling are excellent ways for you to learn. You love to have fun and play with ideas. Any material to be learned has to have some significance for you personally, or add to your self-esteem, otherwise you rapidly lose interest. You learn by acting out the new information, either physically or in your imagination. The most efficient way of succeeding in any goal is to make first a mental picture of your having achieved it. This is called mental rehearsal and is used by many top sportsmen and women as a technique to help improve their performance. You do this spontaneously, as your imagination is your greatest mental asset. You can run through future scenarios in your mind's eye and see, instantly, where a particular piece of information or situation could lead and spot possibilities that other people couldn't even begin to dream of. You are brilliant at coming up with flashes of inspiration for creative breakthroughs and crisis management.

Mercury in Earth: Practical

Endless presentations of feelings, theories and possibilities can make your eyes glaze over and your brain ache to shut down. What really turns you on is trying out these theories and possibilities to see if they work in practice. If they don't, you'll tend to classify them 'of no further interest'.

Emotionally charged information is at best a puzzling non-starter and at worst an irritating turn-off. Practical demonstrations, tried and tested facts and working models fascinate you. Hands-on learning, where you can see how a process functions from start to finish, especially if it leads to some useful material end-product, is right up your street. It's important to allow yourself plenty of time when you are learning, writing or thinking out what to say, otherwise you can feel rushed and out of control, never pleasant sensations for earth signs. Your special skill is in coming up with effective solutions to practical problems and in formulating long-range plans that bring concrete, measurable results.

Mercury in Air: Logical

You love learning about, and playing with, ideas, theories and principles. Often you do this best by arguing or bouncing ideas off other people, or by writing down your thoughts. Your special gift is in your ability to stand back and work out the patterns of relationship between people or things. You much prefer it when facts are presented to you logically and unemotionally and have very little time for the irrational, uncertainty or for personal opinions. You do, though, tend to have plenty of those kinds of views yourself, only you call them logical conclusions. Whether a fact is useful or not is less important than whether it fits into your mental map of how the world operates. If facts don't fit in, you'll either ignore them, find a way of making them fit, or, occasionally, make a grand leap to a new, upgraded theory. Yours is the mind of the scientist or chess player. You make a brilliant planner because you can be detached enough to take an overview of the entire situation.

Mercury in Water: Impressionable

Your mind is sensitive to atmospheres and emotional undertones and to the context in which information is presented. Plain facts and figures can often leave you cold and even intimidated. You can take things too personally and read between the lines for what you believe is really being said or taught. If you don't feel emotionally safe, you can be cautious about revealing your true thoughts. It may be hard, or even impossible, for you to learn properly in what you sense is a hostile environment. You are excellent at impression management. Like a skilful artist painting a picture, you can influence others to think what you'd like them to by using suggestive gestures or pauses and intonations. People with Mercury in water signs are often seriously disadvantaged by left-brain schooling methods that are too rigidly structured for them. You take in information best through pictures or images, so that you get a 'feel' for the material and can make an emotional bond with it, in the same way you connect with people. In emotionally supportive situations where there is a rapport between you and your instructors, or your learning material, you are able just to drink in and absorb circulating knowledge without conscious effort, sometimes not even being clear about how or why you know certain things.

Finding Your Mercury Sign

If you don't yet know your Mercury sign, you might like to see if you can guess what it is from the descriptions below before checking it out in the tables on pp. 113–15.

Sun in Virgo with Mercury in Leo

Patsy Cline	Muriel Gray	Michael Jackson
Dorothy Parker	John Peel	Peter Sellers

The combination of Virgo's sharp observations and the Leo flair for drama can make you a sparkling wit. It would be an unwise person, however, who got on your wrong side by either criticising or upstaging you. There's an edge to your tongue that can be sharp and even merciless. Dorothy Parker, the American critic and humorist, was skilled at playing with words, often to startling effect. 'You can lead a whore to culture,' she once remarked, 'but you cannot make her think.' Talking of her abortion, she said ruefully, 'It serves me right for putting all my eggs in one bastard.'

You're drawn to analyse and talk about your own life. Commentators with this placement, like John Peel and Muriel Gray, report on the world scene from their own very personal perspectives, frequently using incidents from their own lives as illustrations. You may identify so strongly with your views and ideas that you could regard those who disagree with you as making a personal attack on you, or at least being disappointingly disloyal. As you are prone to self-criticism, in extreme cases this can lead to public displays of self-flagellation and tortured self-dissection. There is a tension between your natural reticence and modesty and the need to talk about yourself and even highlight and blow your own trumpet about your own skills and achievements. This combination often works best when you can find a worthwhile cause that you can identify with, and then use your gift for dramatic presentation to further your work and understand yourself better as well. When your heart is focused on healing and helping, and not hurting yourself or others inadvertently, through destructive criticism, you can make a powerfully positive impact on the lives of all you touch.

Sun in Virgo with Mercury in Virgo

Kate Adie	John Buchan	Shirley Conran
Stephen Fry	D.H. Lawrence	Mary Renault

Your approach to any task or learning situation is systematic, breaking the matter down into small, workable units that can then be ticked off your checklists as you go along. Precision, concision and accuracy matter and listeners can often be left with the sense that there are neatly pigeon-holed footnotes and qualifying sentences lurking at the back of your mind, ready to be pulled out as clarification should there be any hairs in need of splitting. Your preferred writing style is lucid, delicate and detailed, threaded together in a logical and orderly fashion. Although there can be a danger of plodding into dullness by being over-pedantic, people with this combination usually have finely tuned and clever wits. Any book by Stephen Fry is testimony to that.

You notice what could be useful and you'll squirrel away in your memory titbits of practical information that might come in handy at a later date. Shirley Conran wrote the bestselling book *Superwoman* on the grounds that life is too short to stuff a mushroom. This is a gold mine of tried-and-tested tips and lists, gathered over the years from first-hand experience, for efficient household management, a Virgo's idea of heaven – and a more spontaneous sign's nightmare.

While you might enjoy examining a theory, especially to check it out for flaws and inconsistencies, and leaps of faith could entertain you briefly, unless there is data that can be put to work, ideas alone won't hold your attention. Appeals to you using emotional language are a complete waste of time. You can have almost endless patience to teach self-help techniques to those who are willing to learn – and to work – but spongers and wasters can expect extremely short shrift from you.

Sun in Virgo with Mercury in Libra

Richard Attenborough	Cherie Blair	Roald Dahl
Queen Elizabeth I	Derek Nimmo	Twiggy

With your charm and diplomacy, you rarely need to resort to direct confrontation, which is fortunate, as you dislike unpleasantness. However, you dislike injustice even more and will use your considerable verbal skills to do what you can to right such wrongs. You are a skilled debater – in fact, you learn best by putting out an idea or an opinion, and seeing how it is received. Often you don't know what you think until you've aired a variety of positions and finally come to the one that seems to be the most balanced. You can find just the right words to be a diplomatic peacemaker, but you may have to be careful not to say what people want to hear, just to please them. You are excellent at strategic thinking and planning because you're capable of taking in the whole situation, and seeing everyone's point of view. This makes you an excellent negotiator and advocate. Cherie Blair, wife of Prime Minister Tony Blair, is one of Britain's most highly paid lawyers, with a first-class mind and keen sense of justice.

Your language often contains a hint of flirtatiousness so you manage to get things done your way with the minimum of offence and the maximum of efficiency. You can be flattering and gently persuasive and may often use other people's names to attract their attention, as if to assure them that you are on their side. When you want your own way, this may not always be entirely sincere. Your tendency to shine the best possible light on difficult situations can make you appear rather naive and idealistic, but you're equally adept at switching sides and stirring up opposition if everything gets too cosy and nice.

NINE

Venus — At Your Pleasure

♀ THE GLYPH FOR VENUS IS MADE UP OF THE CIRCLE OF ETERNITY on top of the cross of matter. Esoterically this represents love, which is a quality of the divine, revealed on earth through personal choice. The saying 'One man's meat is another man's poison' couldn't be more relevant when it comes to what we love. It is a mystery why we find one thing attractive and another unattractive, or even repulsive. Looking at the sign, aspects and house of your Venus can't give any explanation of this mystery, but it can give some clear indications of what it is that you value and find desirable. This can be quite different from what current fashion tells you you should like. For example, many people are strongly turned on by voluptuous bodies but the media constantly shows images of near-anorexics as the desirable ideal. If you ignore what you, personally, find beautiful and try to be, or to love, what at heart leaves you cold, you are setting yourself up for unnecessary pain and dissatisfaction. Being true to your Venus sign, even if other people think you are strange, brings joy and pleasure. It also builds up your self-esteem because it grounds you solidly in your own personal values. This, in turn, makes you much more attractive to others. Not only that, it improves your relationships immeasurably, because you are living authentically and not betraying yourself by trying to prove your worth to others by being something you are not.

Glittering Venus, the brightest planet in the heavens, was named after the goddess of love, war and victory. Earlier names for her were Aphrodite, Innana and Ishtar. She was beautiful, self-willed and self-indulgent but was also skilled in all the arts of civilisation.

Your Venus sign shows what you desire and would like to possess, not only in relationships but also in all aspects of your taste, from clothes and culture to hobbies and hobby-horses. It identifies how and where you can be charming and seductive and skilful at creating your own type of beauty yourself. It also describes your style of attracting partners and the kind of people that turn you on. When your Venus is activated you feel powerful, desirable and wonderfully, wickedly indulged and indulgent. When it is not, even if someone has all the right credentials to make a good match, the relationship will always lack that certain something. If you don't take the chance to express your Venus to a good enough degree somewhere in your life, you miss out woefully on delight and happiness.

Morning Star, Evening Star

Venus appears in the sky either in the morning or in the evening. The ancients launched their attacks when Venus became a morning star, believing that she was then in her warrior-goddess role, releasing aggressive energy for victory in battle. If you're a morning-star person, you're likely to be impulsive, self-willed and idealistic, prepared to hold out until you find the partner who is just right for you.

Relationships and business dealings of morning-star Venus people are said to prosper best whenever Venus in the sky is a morning star. If you are an early bird, you can check this out. At these times Venus can be seen in the eastern sky before the Sun has risen.

The name for Venus as an evening star is Hesperus and it was then, traditionally, said to be sacred to lovers. Evening-star people tend to be easy-going and are open to negotiation, conciliation and making peace. If you are an evening-star Venus person, your best times in relationship and business affairs are said to be when Venus can be seen, jewel-like, in the western sky after the Sun has set.

Because the orbit of Venus is so close to the Sun, your Venus can only be in one of five signs. You have a morning-star Venus if your Venus is in one of the two signs that come before your Sun sign in the zodiac. You have an evening-star Venus if your Venus is in either of the two signs that follow your Sun sign. If you have Venus in the same sign as your Sun, you could be either, depending on whether your Venus is ahead of or behind your Sun. (You can find out which at the author's website www.janeridderpatrick.com.)

If you don't yet know your Venus sign, you might like to read through all of the following descriptions and see if you can guess what it is. You can find out for sure on pp. 116–18

At the beginning of each section are the names of some well-known Virgos with that particular Venus sign. You can find out more about them in Chapter Ten, Famous Virgo Birthdays.

Sun in Virgo with Venus in Cancer

Edward Burne-Jones   Pauline Collins   Cameron Diaz
Lady Antonia Fraser   Macaulay Culkin   Grace Metalious

Home matters to you and you'll take great pleasure in
making sure that yours is not only comfortable but
beautiful and efficient too. You're at your happiest and
most secure in the company of those you consider your own
special family – whether this means a few familiar
companions or your extended clan of birth. The ordinary
and intimate details of the lives and histories of those you
feel connected to fascinate you. Following them avidly gives
you a sense of belonging – like being immersed in a soap
opera. Grace Metalious's *Peyton Place*, a tale of small-town
sex and scandal, was in fact TV's first major soap.

Man or woman, you like to mother and be mothered by
your partner. That doesn't mean communicating in baby
talk, it means knowing you can lean on each other for
support through good times and bad and that you accept
each other, warts and all, just exactly as you are. With your
need to be of service and ability to tune in to other people's
feelings, take care not to get so entangled in sorting out
other people's problems that you neglect yourself, and end
up resentful. You are so impressionable and self-critical that
if anybody dislikes or snubs you, you take it to heart. This
can sap your self-confidence badly. It's vital to cultivate
people who appreciate, value and adore you – and whom
you can appreciate in turn without your critical mind and
tongue intruding too much. Often you prefer the known
and familiar to the unknown, so an adventurous and
protective partner who will coax you out into the wider
world from time to time could be perfect for you.

Sun in Virgo with Venus in Leo

| Lauren Bacall | John Buchan | Greta Garbo |
| Jeremy Irons | Zandra Rhodes | Raine Spencer |

You love to express your theatrical streak, though you may not go to such extremes as the fashion designer Zandra Rhodes, whose eye-popping designs, pink hair and earrings the size of dinner plates are hard to overlook. With your star quality, you need to find just the right situations to bridge that gap between your innate modesty and your love of the flamboyant or ceremonial.

Even if your taste is somewhat more restrained, you combine an eye for detail and a shrewd sense of dramatic timing which ensures that, when you so choose, the eyes of the world are on you, admiring. Quality impresses you but the Virgo–Leo combination demands both class and cleanliness. Raine, Countess Spencer, horrified her step-family when she insisted on replacing some of the tattered and faded silk hangings and chair covers at the Spencer stately home, despite the fact that they were much-loved antiques.

As prestige matters to you, it's essential you can be proud of your partner, but you do like to be seen to be special yourself. A consort who gets more than their fair share of what you see as your limelight could quickly fall out of favour. You love what is honourable, noble and generous. Developing those qualities in yourself will bring you enormous satisfaction and improve the quality of all of your relationships. It will help tone down possible friction produced by compounding Virgo criticism with Leo bossiness, a mix that can sometimes be less than charitable. At best, like the writer John Buchan, you can combine a generosity of heart and cleverness of wit to speak the truth about others with compassion and humour.

Sun in Virgo with Venus in Virgo

Richard Attenborough	Anne Bancroft	Ingrid Bergman
A.S. Byatt	Sophia Loren	Michael Ondaatje

You need a partner whose mind and professionalism you can admire and respect, especially for their wit, skill and fastidious taste. It is best if your work goals dovetail but don't clash or compete. Some with this placement go into relationships that are purely functional, based on practical considerations rather than passion or even love. It is not always easy for you to show your affection spontaneously and openly, so sometimes others see you as rather aloof and even a little cold. You are willing to work on relationships that you believe are worthwhile and, like everything else in your life, once you've learned the ropes of how to go about it, you can become skilled as a lover and partner. Deep down there is a well of powerful sensuality that can be tapped when circumstances are right and you feel safe and cherished. Then you can light up and surprise others by the intensity of your desires and the matter-of-factness with which you follow them, regardless of what anyone has to say about it.

You take enormous pleasure in work well done. Richard Attenborough's films are always detailed, beautiful to look at and full of outstanding performances. One of the greatest challenges is learning how to deal with a tendency to criticise yourself and others. You can't help noticing imperfections but that doesn't mean that you need to comment on them. Biting your tongue on those helpful or critical remarks can save your relationships a great deal of stress. With your Virgo realism, you can learn to accept that nothing and nobody is perfect and then work with compassion to change what you are invited to change, and to leave well alone what you aren't.

Sun in Virgo with Venus in Libra

Laura Ashley	Sean Connery	Queen Elizabeth I
Stephen Fry	Hugh Grant	Claudia Schiffer

There can be a conflict between your strong desire for partnership and an equally powerful need to spend much of your time alone. With an eye for detail and an appreciation of elegance, you like to be beautifully turned out. A man with this placement can enjoy being a bit of a dandy. Teasing and flirting come easily and you're an expert flatterer.

Your love of fairness means that you are always ready to listen to everyone's opinions, but if things become overly nice and polite, you'll enjoy stirring up some mischief. There's nothing you like better than a good debate, as long as it doesn't turn heavy and nasty. You'll put your money where your mouth is, though, if you become politically involved in righting what you see as wrongs. It's important that you sense you are liked and supported because disharmony or gross behaviour of any kind can make you deeply unhappy, but be careful not to be swayed from your own good judgement just to give the impression of being Ms or Mr Nice.

Culture, civilisation and all that is fine and gracious in life fill you with pleasure. Think of the blossoming of culture in the reign of Queen Elizabeth I. Your partner of choice is elegant, intelligent and easy on the eye, but you may be a little naive and idealistic about relationships, expecting to ride off into the sunset where unruffled happiness awaits you ever after. Once you've had a few brushes with the facts of life, especially that other people are not always fair-minded and unselfish, your Virgo realism can help you make the most of this utterly charming combination.

Sun in Virgo with Venus in Scorpio

Cherie Blair	Francis Chichester	Agatha Christie
Michael Faraday	Gustav Holst	Twiggy

Beneath that seemingly millpond-smooth exterior beats a passionate and sometimes jealous heart. You are intensely private and may be secretive about what is really going on in your life. There can be much agony and ecstasy behind closed doors. Agatha Christie was deserted by her first husband for another woman, and her second, who was much younger than her, is reported to have had several affairs. She lived out the Scorpionic love of sex, death and mystery through her detective stories.

You have no time for superficiality and love to push yourself to the limits. You'll throw yourself into work with a passion, toiling away relentlessly until the task is done – properly. Power always comes into your life, or love formula, in one way or other. There's something about it, and wealth too, which turns you on, and either you'll attract money and power yourself or find a partner who does – or both. Your partner may be influential, either personally or in position, and may be intense and rather uncompromising. Occasionally this placement can indicate abusive relationships, and if you have experienced something of the sort, know that you don't have to be a doormat or love slave. Nor do you have to put up with, or create, the love triangles that are another familiar feature of Venus in Scorpio. Extremes excite you, and it can be hard to give up the adrenaline rush that comes with cliff-hanging situations. Part of this urge comes from the fact that you're looking for total emotional security and are prone to testing your partner to see if he or she really does care. Once you're sure your mate is trustworthy, you are capable of intense loyalty forever and ever. Amen.

TEN

Famous Virgo Birthdays

FIND OUT WHO SHARES YOUR MOON, MERCURY AND VENUS SIGNS, and any challenging Sun aspects, and see what they have done with the material they were born with. Notice how often it is not just the personalities of the people themselves but the roles of actors, characters of authors and works of artists that reflect their astrological make-up. In reading standard biographies, I've been constantly astounded – and, of course, delighted – at how often phrases used to describe individuals could have been lifted straight from their astrological profiles. Check it out yourself!

A few people below have been given a choice of two Moons. This is because the Moon changed sign on the day that they were born and no birth time was available. You may be able to guess which one is correct if you read the descriptions of the Moon signs in Chapter Seven.

22 August
1893 Dorothy Parker, American journalist with biting acidic wit
Sun aspects: none
Moon: Capricorn   Mercury: Leo   Venus: Libra

23 August
1950 Edson Queiroz, Brazilian psychic surgeon apparently operating with his bare hands
Sun aspects: none
Moon: Capricorn   Mercury: Virgo   Venus: Leo

24 August
1759 William Wilberforce, philanthropist who abolished the British slave trade
Sun aspects: none
Moon: Virgo   Mercury: Virgo   Venus: Libra

25 August
1930 Sean Connery, versatile Scottish actor and the definitive James Bond
Sun aspects: Neptune
Moon: Virgo   Mercury: Virgo   Venus: Libra

26 August
1875 John Buchan, prolific writer, poet and statesman, *The Thirty-Nine Steps*
Sun aspects: Pluto
Moon: Gemini   Mercury: Virgo   Venus: Leo

27 August
1932 Lady Antonia Fraser, poet and historical biographer, *Mary Queen of Scots*
Sun aspects: Neptune
Moon: Cancer   Mercury: Leo   Venus: Cancer

28 August
1749 Johann Wolfgang von Goethe, German poet and scientist, *Faust*
Sun aspects: Pluto
Moon: Pisces   Mercury: Leo   Venus: Virgo

29 August
1958 Michael Jackson, multimillionaire singer and plastic surgery enthusiast
Sun aspects: Pluto
Moon: Pisces   Mercury: Leo   Venus: Leo

30 August
1797 Mary Shelley, author of *Frankenstein*
Sun aspects: Uranus, Pluto
Moon: Sagittarius   Mercury: Virgo   Venus: Libra

31 August
1870 Maria Montessori, founder of the Montessori education system
Sun aspects: none
Moon: Scorpio   Mercury: Libra   Venus: Leo

1 September
1875 Edgar Rice Burroughs, author and creator of Tarzan, Lord of the Jungle
Sun aspects: none
Moon: Libra   Mercury: Virgo   Venus: Virgo

2 September

1964 Keanu Reaves, inscrutable actor, *The Matrix*, *The Devil's Advocate*
Sun aspects: Saturn, Uranus, Pluto
Moon: Cancer   Mercury: Virgo   Venus: Cancer

3 September

1940 Pauline Collins, actress and star of *Shirley Valentine*
Sun aspects: none
Moon: Libra   Mercury: Virgo   Venus: Cancer

4 September

1905 Mary Renault, historical novelist, *The King Must Die*
Sun aspects: none
Moon: Scorpio   Mercury: Virgo   Venus: Leo

5 September

1946 Freddie Mercury, incomparable lead singer of Queen, who died of AIDS
Sun aspects: Uranus
Moon: Sagittarius   Mercury: Virgo   Venus: Libra

6 September

1888 Joseph Kennedy, financier and founder of the US Kennedy political clan
Sun aspects: Pluto
Moon: Virgo   Mercury: Virgo   Venus: Virgo

7 September

1533 Queen Elizabeth I of England, known as the Virgin Queen
Sun aspects: Neptune
Moon: Taurus   Mercury: Libra   Venus: Libra

8 September
1925 Peter Sellers, comedian and actor of eccentric roles, *Dr Strangelove*
Sun aspects: Uranus
Moon: Taurus   Mercury: Leo   Venus: Libra

9 September
1960 Hugh Grant, English actor, *Four Weddings and a Funeral*
Sun aspects: none
Moon: Taurus   Mercury: Virgo   Venus: Libra

10 September
1943 Neale Donald Walsch, author of the bestselling *Conversations with God*
Sun aspects: Saturn, Uranus
Moon: Capricorn   Mercury: Libra   Venus: Virgo

11 September
1885 D.H. Lawrence, novelist, *Lady Chatterley's Lover*, *Sons and Lovers*
Sun aspects: none
Moon: Libra   Mercury: Virgo   Venus: Libra

12 September
1913 Jesse Owens, outstanding black Olympic athlete, snubbed by Hitler
Sun aspects: Saturn
Moon: Aquarius   Mercury: Virgo   Venus: Leo

13 September

1916 Roald Dahl, children's writer, *Charlie and the Chocolate Factory*
Sun aspects: none
Moon: Aries   Mercury: Libra   Venus: Leo

14 September

1879 Margaret Sanger, nurse and feminist jailed for advocating birth control
Sun aspects: none
Moon: Leo   Mercury: Virgo   Venus: Libra

15 September

1890 Agatha Christie, detective novelist, creator of Hercule Poirot and Miss Marple
Sun aspects: none
Moon: Libra   Mercury: Libra   Venus: Scorpio

16 September

1924 Lauren Baccall, husky-voiced actress, *To Have and Have Not*
Sun aspects: Uranus
Moon: Aries   Mercury: Virgo   Venus: Leo

17 September

1901 Sir Francis Chichester, winner of the first solo transatlantic yacht race
Sun aspects: Neptune, Pluto
Moon: Scorpio   Mercury: Libra   Venus: Scorpio

18 September
1905 Greta Garbo, enigmatic and aloof Swedish actress, 'I want to be left alone'
Sun aspects: Uranus, Pluto
Moon: Taurus   Mercury: Virgo   Venus: Leo

19 September
1945 Kate Adie, TV journalist showing cool professionalism in the face of danger
Sun aspects: Uranus, Neptune
Moon: Aquarius   Mercury: Virgo   Venus: Leo

20 September
1934 Sophia Loren, sultry Italian actress, *The Millionairess*
Sun aspects: none
Moon: Aquarius   Mercury: Libra   Venus: Virgo

21 September
1947 Stephen King, prolific writer of horror stories, *The Shining*, *Carrie*
Sun aspects: Uranus
Moon: Sagittarius   Mercury: Libra   Venus: Libra

22 September
1791 Michael Faraday, one of the greatest original scientists ever
Sun aspects: none
Moon: Cancer   Mercury: Libra   Venus: Scorpio

23 September
Cherie Blair, lawyer and wife of British Prime Minister Tony Blair
Sun aspects: Uranus
Moon: Taurus   Mercury: Libra   Venus: Leo

Other Virgo people mentioned in this book
Jonathan Aitken, prominent politician, jailed for perjury ☆ Prince Albert, consort of Queen Victoria ☆ Martin Amis, novelist, *Money* ☆ Laura Ashley, designer of nostalgic country fashions ☆ Richard Attenborough, actor and film director, *Gandhi* ☆ Anne Bancroft, actress, Mrs Robinson in *The Graduate* ☆ Martin Bell, BBC correspondent and anti-sleaze MP ☆ Ingrid Bergman, actress, *Casablanca* ☆ Bruno Bettelheim, child psychiatrist, *The Uses of Enchantment* ☆ Edward Burne-Jones, pre-Raphaelite painter and stained-glass window artist ☆ A.S. Byatt, author, *Possession* ☆ Patsy Cline, singer, 'I Fall to Pieces' ☆ Leonard Cohen, singer and songwriter, 'Suzanne' ☆ Shirley Conran, writer, *Superwoman* ☆ Macaulay Culkin, actor, *Home Alone* ☆ Cameron Diaz, actress, *Charlie's Angels* ☆ 'Mama' Cass Elliot, singer in The Mamas and The Papas, 'California Dreamin'' ☆ Frederick Forsyth, author, *The Day of the Jackal* ☆ Stephen Fry, actor, humorist and writer, *The Liar* ☆ William Golding, author, *Lord of the Flies* ☆ Muriel Gray, journalist ☆ Prince Harry, second son of Prince Charles and the late Princess Diana ☆ Lenny Henry, stand-up comedian ☆ James Hilton, author, *Lost Horizon* ☆ Buddy Holly, singer, 'That'll be the Day' ☆ Gustav Holst, composer, *The Planets* ☆ Jeremy Irons, actor, *Brideshead Revisited* ☆ Michael Jackson, superstar singer, *Thriller* ☆ Arthur Koestler, author, *Darkness at Noon* ☆ Lady Elizabeth Longford, royal biographer, *Queen Victoria* ☆ King Ludwig II of Bavaria, builder of fantastical castles ☆ Alexander McCall Smith, author, *The No.1 Ladies' Detective Agency* ☆ Grace Metalious, author, *Peyton Place* ☆ Jessica Mitford, writer and critic, *The*

American Way of Death ☆ Kenneth More, actor, *The Thirty-Nine Steps* ☆ Van Morrison, singer, 'Brown Eyed Girl' ☆ Grandma Moses, American folk artist ☆ Beverly Nichols, writer, *Down the Garden Path* ☆ Derek Nimmo, actor, *Oh Brother!* ☆ Jessye Norman, opera diva ☆ Michael Ondaatje, author, *The English Patient* ☆ John Peel, broadcaster, *Home Truths* ☆ Alan Pinkerton, founder of the Pinkerton Detective Agency ☆ Man Ray, surrealist photographer ☆ Zandra Rhodes, fashion designer ☆ Jean Rhys, author, *Wide Sargasso Sea* ☆ Siegfried Sassoon, war poet, *Survivors* ☆ Elsa Schiaparelli, fashion designer ☆ Claudia Schiffer, supermodel ☆ Clara Schumann, pianist and wife of the composer Robert Schumann ☆ Harry Secombe, singer and comedian, *The Goon Show* ☆ Upton Sinclair, author and social critic, *The Jungle* ☆ Raine Spencer, stepmother of Princess Diana ☆ Graham Sutherland, controversial post-war painter ☆ Mother Teresa, nun who won a Nobel Peace Prize for her work in the Calcutta slums ☆ Margaret Trudeau, ex-wife of President Trudeau of Canada ☆ Twiggy, model who was the face and figure of the 1960s ☆ Dinah Washington, jazz singer nicknamed Queen of the Blues ☆ Raquel Welch, actress, *One Million Years BC* ☆ H.G. Wells, author, *The Time Machine* ☆ Jimmy Young, radio DJ

ELEVEN

Finding Your Sun, Moon, Mercury and Venus Signs

All of the astrological data in this book was calculated by Astrolabe, who also supply a wide range of astrological software. I am most grateful for their help and generosity.

ASTROLABE, PO Box 1750, Brewster, MA 02631, USA
www.alabe.com

PLEASE NOTE THAT ALL OF THE TIMES GIVEN ARE IN GREENWICH MEAN TIME (GMT). If you were born during British Summer Time (BST) you will need to subtract one hour from your birth time to convert it to GMT. If you were born outside of the British Isles, find the time zone of your place of birth and the number of hours it is different from GMT. Add the difference in hours if you were born west of the UK, and subtract the difference if you were born east of the UK to convert your birth time to GMT.

Your Sun Sign

Check your year of birth, and if you were born between the dates and times given the Sun was in Virgo when you were born – confirming that you're a Virgo. If you were born before the time on the date that Virgo begins in your year, you are a Leo. If you were born after the time on the date Virgo ends in your year, you are a Libran.

Your Moon Sign

The Moon changes sign every two and a half days. To find your Moon sign, first find your year of birth. You will notice that in each year box there are three columns.

The second column shows the day of the month that the Moon changed sign, while the first column gives the abbreviation for the sign that the Moon entered on that date.

In the middle column, the month has been omitted, so that the dates run from, for example, 23 to 31 (August) and then from 1 to 23 (September).

In the third column, after the star, the time that the Moon changed sign on that day is given.

Look down the middle column of your year box to find your date of birth. If your birth date is given, look to the third column to find the time that the Moon changed sign. If you were born after that time, your Moon sign is given in the first column next to your birth date. If you were born before that time, your Moon sign is the one above the one next to your birth date.

If your birth date is not given, find the closest date before it. The sign shown next to that date is your Moon sign.

If you were born on a day that the Moon changed signs and you do not know your time of birth, try out both of that day's Moon signs and feel which one fits you best.

The abbreviations for the signs are as follows:

Aries – Ari   Taurus – Tau   Gemini – Gem   Cancer – Can
Leo – Leo   Virgo – Vir   Libra – Lib   Scorpio – Sco
Sagittarius – Sag Capricorn – Cap   Aquarius – Aqu   Pisces – Pis

Your Mercury Sign

Find your year of birth and then the column in which your
birthday falls. Look up to the top of the column to find
your Mercury sign. You will see that some dates appear
twice. This is because Mercury changed sign that day. If
your birthday falls on one of these dates, try out both
Mercury signs and see which one fits you best. If you know
your birth time, you can find out for sure which Mercury
sign is yours on my website – www.janeridderpatrick.com.

Your Venus Sign

Find your year of birth and then the column in which your
birthday falls. Look up to the top of the column to find
your Venus sign. Some dates have two possible signs. That's
because Venus changed signs that day. Try them both out
and see which fits you best. If the year you are interested in
doesn't appear in the tables, or you have Venus in the same
sign as your Sun and want to know whether you have a
morning or evening star Venus, you can find the
information on my website – www.janeridderpatrick.com.

♍ Virgo Sun Tables ☉

YEAR	VIRGO BEGINS	VIRGO ENDS
1930	23 Aug 15.41	23 Sep 18.35
1931	24 Aug 03.10	24 Sep 00.23
1932	23 Aug 09.06	23 Sep 06.15
1933	23 Aug 14.52	23 Sep 12.01
1934	23 Aug 20.32	23 Sep 17.45
1935	24 Aug 02.23	23 Sep 23.38
1936	23 Aug 08.10	23 Sep 05.25
1937	23 Aug 13.57	23 Sep 11.12
1938	23 Aug 19.45	23 Sep 16.59
1939	24 Aug 01.31	23 Sep 22.49
1940	23 Aug 07.28	23 Sep 04.45
1941	23 Aug 13.16	23 Sep 10.32
1942	23 Aug 18.58	23 Sep 16.16
1943	24 Aug 00.54	23 Sep 22.11
1944	23 Aug 06.46	23 Sep 04.01
1945	23 Aug 12.35	23 Sep 09.49
1946	23 Aug 18.26	23 Sep 15.40
1947	24 Aug 00.08	23 Sep 21.28
1948	23 Aug 06.02	23 Sep 03.21
1949	23 Aug 11.48	23 Sep 09.05
1950	23 Aug 17.23	23 Sep 14.43
1951	23 Aug 23.16	23 Sep 20.36
1952	23 Aug 05.02	23 Sep 02.23
1953	23 Aug 10.45	23 Sep 08.05
1954	23 Aug 16.35	23 Sep 13.55
1955	23 Aug 22.18	23 Sep 19.40
1956	23 Aug 04.14	23 Sep 07.26
1957	23 Aug 10.07	23 Sep 07.26
1958	23 Aug 15.45	23 Sep 13.08
1959	23 Aug 21.43	23 Sep 19.08
1960	23 Aug 03.34	23 Sep 00.58
1961	23 Aug 09.18	23 Sep 06.42
1962	23 Aug 15.12	23 Sep 12.35
1963	23 Aug 20.57	23 Sep 18.23

YEAR	VIRGO BEGINS	VIRGO ENDS
1964	23 Aug 02.50	23 Sep 00.16
1965	23 Aug 08.42	23 Sep 06.05
1966	23 Aug 14.17	23 Sep 11.43
1967	23 Aug 20.12	23 Sep 17.37
1968	23 Aug 02.02	22 Sep 23.26
1969	23 Aug 07.43	23 Sep 05.06
1970	23 Aug 13.33	23 Sep 10.58
1971	23 Aug 19.15	23 Sep 16.44
1972	23 Aug 01.02	22 Sep 22.32
1973	23 Aug 06.53	23 Sep 04.21
1974	23 Aug 12.28	23 Sep 09.58
1975	23 Aug 18.23	23 Sep 15.55
1976	23 Aug 00.18	22 Sep 21.48
1977	23 Aug 06.00	23 Sep 03.29
1978	23 Aug 11.56	23 Sep 09.25
1979	23 Aug 17.46	23 Sep 15.16
1980	22 Aug 23.40	22 Sep 03.05
1981	23 Aug 05.38	23 Sep 03.05
1982	23 Aug 11.15	23 Sep 08.46
1983	23 Aug 17.07	23 Sep 14.41
1984	22 Aug 23.00	22 Sep 20.32
1985	23 Aug 04.35	23 Sep 02.07
1986	23 Aug 10.25	23 Sep 07.58
1987	23 Aug 16.09	23 Sep 13.45
1988	22 Aug 21.54	22 Sep 19.28
1989	23 Aug 03.46	23 Sep 01.19
1990	23 Aug 09.20	23 Sep 06.55
1991	23 Aug 15.12	23 Sep 18.42
1992	22 Aug 21.10	22 Sep 18.42
1993	23 Aug 02.50	23 Sep 00.22
1994	23 Aug 08.43	23 Sep 06.19
1995	23 Aug 14.34	23 Sep 12.12
1996	22 Aug 20.22	22 Sep 18.00
1997	23 Aug 02.19	22 Sep 23.55
1998	23 Aug 07.58	23 Sep 05.37
1999	23 Aug 13.51	23 Sep 11.31
2000	22 Aug 19.48	22 Sep 17.27

♍ Virgo – Finding Your Moon Sign ☽

1930		
Vir	24	*03:13
Lib	26	*02:58
Sco	28	*05:10
Sag	30	*11:05
Cap	1	*20:35
Aqu	4	*08:27
Pis	6	*21:06
Ari	9	*09:20
Tau	11	*20:17
Gem	14	*05:00
Can	16	*10:41
Leo	18	*13:17
Vir	20	*13:45
Lib	22	*13:44

1931		
Aqu	25	*08:38
Pis	27	*19:27
Ari	30	*07:56
Tau	1	*20:58
Gem	4	*08:42
Can	6	*17:14
Leo	8	*21:46
Vir	10	*23:03
Lib	12	*22:43
Sco	14	*22:41
Sag	17	*00:40
Cap	19	*05:47
Aqu	21	*14:18

1932		
Gem	24	*05:33
Can	26	*16:49
Leo	29	*01:01
Vir	31	*05:58
Lib	2	*08:31
Sco	4	*10:06
Sag	6	*12:00
Cap	8	*15:11
Aqu	10	*20:16
Pis	13	*03:31
Ari	15	*13:01
Tau	18	*00:33
Gem	20	*13:13

1933		
Lib	23	*17:29
Sco	25	*22:43
Sag	28	*02:20
Cap	30	*04:51
Aqu	1	*06:59
Pis	3	*09:44
Ari	5	*14:15
Tau	7	*21:35
Gem	10	*08:00
Can	12	*20:24
Leo	15	*08:29
Vir	17	*18:13
Lib	20	*00:50
Sco	22	*04:59

1934		
Pis	24	*18:07
Ari	26	*18:43
Tau	28	*21:55
Gem	31	*04:55
Can	2	*15:40
Leo	5	*04:31
Vir	7	*17:16
Lib	10	*04:22
Sco	12	*13:18
Sag	14	*20:02
Cap	17	*00:34
Aqu	19	*03:05
Pis	21	*04:13

♍ Virgo – Finding Your Moon Sign ☽

1935		
Can	23	*16:17
Leo	26	*03:00
Vir	28	*15:20
Lib	31	*04:07
Sco	2	*16:21
Sag	5	*02:47
Cap	7	*10:06
Aqu	9	*13:42
Pis	11	*14:14
Ari	13	*13:20
Tau	15	*13:11
Gem	17	*15:48
Can	19	*22:28
Leo	22	*08:50

1936		
Sag	25	*02:08
Cap	27	*12:33
Aqu	29	*19:11
Pis	31	*22:04
Ari	2	*22:42
Tau	4	*23:04
Gem	7	*00:55
Can	9	*05:15
Leo	11	*12:13
Vir	13	*21:20
Lib	16	*08:12
Sco	18	*20:32
Sag	21	*09:23

1937		
Ari	24	*08:22
Tau	26	*11:56
Gem	28	*15:01
Can	30	*18:03
Leo	1	*21:21
Vir	4	*01:35
Lib	6	*07:48
Sco	8	*16:59
Sag	11	*04:58
Cap	13	*17:51
Aqu	16	*04:50
Pis	18	*12:17
Ari	20	*16:30
Tau	22	*18:49

1938		
Leo	23	*08:26
Vir	25	*08:43
Lib	27	*10:27
Sco	29	*15:26
Sag	1	*00:28
Cap	3	*12:30
Aqu	6	*01:09
Pis	8	*12:27
Ari	10	*21:39
Tau	13	*04:53
Gem	15	*10:22
Can	17	*14:08
Leo	19	*16:25
Vir	21	*18:00

1939		
Cap	24	*10:34
Aqu	26	*22:09
Pis	29	*10:42
Ari	31	*23:14
Tau	3	*10:46
Gem	5	*20:01
Can	8	*01:50
Leo	10	*04:10
Vir	12	*04:08
Lib	14	*03:38
Sco	16	*04:43
Sag	18	*09:02
Cap	20	*17:10

♍ Virgo – Finding Your Moon Sign ☽

1940		
Tau	23	*10:16
Gem	25	*22:11
Can	28	*06:53
Leo	30	*11:29
Vir	1	*12:55
Lib	3	*12:54
Sco	5	*13:17
Sag	7	*15:36
Cap	9	*20:46
Aqu	12	*04:51
Pis	14	*15:25
Ari	17	*03:43
Tau	19	*16:45
Gem	22	*05:05

1941		
Vir	22	*19:52
Lib	24	*23:20
Sco	27	*01:48
Sag	29	*04:12
Cap	31	*07:17
Aqu	2	*11:39
Pis	4	*17:51
Ari	7	*02:29
Tau	9	*13:32
Gem	12	*02:05
Can	14	*14:08
Leo	16	*23:34
Vir	19	*05:28
Lib	21	*08:16

1942		
Aqu	23	*22:07
Pis	25	*23:55
Ari	28	*03:39
Tau	30	*10:30
Gem	1	*20:40
Can	4	*09:00
Leo	6	*21:14
Vir	9	*07:30
Lib	11	*15:04
Sco	13	*20:18
Sag	15	*23:57
Cap	18	*02:47
Aqu	20	*05:27
Pis	22	*08:33

1943		
Can	25	*05:06
Leo	27	*17:49
Vir	30	*06:46
Lib	1	*18:33
Sco	4	*04:19
Sag	6	*11:37
Cap	8	*16:12
Aqu	10	*18:18
Pis	12	*18:46
Ari	14	*19:08
Tau	16	*21:15
Gem	19	*02:43
Can	21	*12:11

1944		
Sco	24	*06:12
Sag	26	*16:51
Cap	29	*00:10
Aqu	31	*03:43
Pis	2	*04:14
Ari	4	*03:27
Tau	6	*03:29
Gem	8	*06:13
Can	10	*12:47
Leo	12	*22:50
Vir	15	*11:00
Lib	17	*23:47
Sco	20	*12:10
Sag	22	*23:15

♍ Virgo – Finding Your Moon Sign ☽

1945			1946			1947			1948			1949		
Pis	23	*12:04	Leo	24	*12:38	Sag	23	*13:35	Tau	25	*01:02	Vir	24	*02:55
Ari	25	*13:29	Vir	26	*15:54	Cap	26	*01:30	Gem	27	*10:38	Lib	26	*03:24
Tau	27	*14:33	Lib	28	*21:15	Aqu	28	*14:17	Can	29	*16:33	Sco	28	*04:19
Gem	29	*16:47	Sco	31	*05:49	Pis	31	*02:02	Leo	31	*18:40	Sag	30	*07:00
Can	31	*21:00	Sag	2	*17:31	Ari	2	*12:01	Vir	2	*18:20	Cap	1	*12:05
Leo	3	*03:19	Cap	5	*06:23	Tau	4	*20:09	Lib	4	*17:35	Aqu	3	*19:37
Vir	5	*11:37	Aqu	7	*17:41	Gem	7	*02:17	Sco	6	*18:34	Pis	6	*05:26
Lib	7	*21:48	Pis	10	*01:44	Can	9	*06:12	Sag	8	*22:52	Ari	8	*17:13
Sco	10	*09:47	Ari	12	*06:48	Leo	11	*08:02	Cap	11	*06:56	Tau	11	*06:12
Sag	12	*22:37	Tau	14	*10:03	Vir	13	*08:50	Aqu	13	*17:58	Gem	13	*18:46
Cap	15	*10:10	Gem	16	*12:45	Lib	15	*10:16	Pis	16	*06:26	Can	16	*04:51
Aqu	17	*18:19	Can	18	*15:41	Sco	17	*14:11	Ari	18	*19:01	Leo	18	*11:03
Pis	19	*22:17	Leo	20	*19:12	Sag	19	*21:50	Tau	21	*06:45	Vir	20	*13:32
Ari	21	*23:10	Vir	22	*23:38	Cap	22	*08:57				Lib	22	*13:41

♍ Virgo – Finding Your Moon Sign ☽

1950		
Aqu	25	*02:53
Pis	27	*08:02
Ari	29	*15:45
Tau	1	*02:19
Gem	3	*14:45
Can	6	*02:52
Leo	8	*12:32
Vir	10	*18:54
Lib	12	*22:27
Sco	15	*00:26
Sag	17	*02:12
Cap	19	*04:48
Aqu	21	*09:00

1951		
Gem	24	*09:27
Can	26	*21:44
Leo	29	*10:09
Vir	31	*20:59
Lib	3	*05:31
Sco	5	*11:47
Sag	7	*16:10
Cap	9	*19:05
Aqu	11	*21:11
Pis	13	*23:22
Ari	16	*02:47
Tau	18	*08:41
Gem	20	*17:46

1952		
Lib	23	*08:41
Sco	25	*19:09
Sag	28	*02:52
Cap	30	*07:23
Aqu	1	*09:02
Pis	3	*08:59
Ari	5	*08:57
Tau	7	*10:49
Gem	9	*16:06
Can	12	*01:24
Leo	14	*13:38
Vir	17	*02:41
Lib	19	*14:40
Sco	22	*00:42

1953		
Pis	24	*18:11
Ari	26	*17:45
Tau	28	*18:09
Gem	30	*21:07
Can	2	*03:30
Leo	4	*13:05
Vir	7	*00:47
Lib	9	*13:27
Sco	12	*02:05
Sag	14	*13:30
Cap	16	*22:19
Aqu	19	*03:28
Pis	21	*05:06

1954		
Can	23	*12:50
Leo	25	*18:22
Vir	28	*01:44
Lib	30	*11:12
Sco	1	*22:48
Sag	4	*11:31
Cap	6	*23:08
Aqu	9	*07:30
Pis	11	*11:53
Ari	13	*13:21
Tau	15	*13:44
Gem	17	*14:55
Can	19	*18:12
Leo	22	*00:04

♍ Virgo – Finding Your Moon Sign ☽

1955		
Sag	25	*06:03
Cap	27	*18:56
Aqu	30	*06:34
Pis	1	*15:22
Ari	3	*21:23
Tau	6	*01:36
Gem	8	*04:58
Can	10	*08:00
Leo	12	*11:02
Vir	14	*14:33
Lib	16	*19:35
Sco	19	*03:19
Sag	21	*14:11

1956		
Ari	24	*02:29
Tau	26	*11:22
Gem	28	*17:59
Can	30	*21:50
Leo	1	*23:13
Vir	3	*23:20
Lib	6	*00:05
Sco	8	*03:27
Sag	10	*10:47
Cap	12	*21:46
Aqu	15	*10:27
Pis	17	*22:32
Ari	20	*08:46
Tau	22	*17:00

1957		
Leo	23	*08:50
Vir	25	*08:25
Lib	27	*07:41
Sco	29	*08:46
Sag	31	*13:08
Cap	2	*21:05
Aqu	5	*07:50
Pis	7	*20:03
Ari	10	*08:44
Tau	12	*20:56
Gem	15	*07:25
Can	17	*14:48
Leo	19	*18:30
Vir	21	*19:10

1958		
Cap	24	*03:38
Aqu	26	*10:28
Pis	28	*19:25
Ari	31	*06:35
Tau	2	*19:23
Gem	5	*08:06
Can	7	*18:21
Leo	10	*00:40
Vir	12	*03:18
Lib	14	*03:44
Sco	16	*03:49
Sag	18	*05:16
Cap	20	*09:13
Aqu	22	*16:03

1959		
Tau	23	*14:58
Gem	26	*03:18
Can	28	*15:32
Leo	31	*01:32
Vir	2	*08:30
Lib	4	*12:55
Sco	6	*15:52
Sag	8	*18:20
Cap	10	*21:04
Aqu	13	*00:43
Pis	15	*05:53
Ari	17	*13:16
Tau	19	*23:12
Gem	22	*11:16

♍ Virgo – Finding Your Moon Sign ☽

1960		
Lib	24	*20:08
Sco	27	*03:22
Sag	29	*08:18
Cap	31	*11:08
Aqu	2	*12:34
Pis	4	*13:51
Ari	6	*16:26
Tau	8	*21:45
Gem	11	*06:31
Can	13	*18:10
Leo	16	*06:46
Vir	18	*18:06
Lib	21	*02:57

1961		
Aqu	23	*23:24
Pis	25	*23:02
Ari	27	*22:49
Tau	30	*00:38
Gem	1	*05:52
Can	3	*15:00
Leo	6	*03:00
Vir	8	*16:04
Lib	11	*04:33
Sco	13	*15:22
Sag	15	*23:53
Cap	18	*05:41
Aqu	20	*08:42
Pis	22	*09:35

1962		
Can	24	*18:33
Leo	27	*03:30
Vir	29	*14:35
Lib	1	*03:00
Sco	3	*15:46
Sag	6	*03:25
Cap	8	*12:18
Aqu	10	*17:25
Pis	12	*19:01
Ari	14	*18:32
Tau	16	*18:00
Gem	18	*19:29
Can	21	*00:26

1963		
Sco	24	*11:39
Sag	27	*00:14
Cap	29	*11:56
Aqu	31	*20:36
Pis	3	*01:35
Ari	5	*03:51
Tau	7	*05:02
Gem	9	*06:45
Can	11	*10:08
Leo	13	*15:30
Vir	15	*22:47
Lib	18	*07:59
Sco	20	*19:10

1964		
Pis	23	*05:13
Ari	25	*12:14
Tau	27	*17:23
Gem	29	*21:15
Can	1	*00:12
Leo	3	*02:36
Vir	5	*05:12
Lib	7	*09:19
Sco	9	*16:20
Sag	12	*02:47
Cap	14	*15:30
Aqu	17	*03:46
Pis	19	*13:21
Ari	21	*19:43

♍ Virgo – Finding Your Moon Sign ☽

1965		
Leo	24	*14:00
Vir	26	*13:36
Lib	28	*13:53
Sco	30	*16:54
Sag	2	*00:00
Cap	4	*10:51
Aqu	6	*23:33
Pis	9	*11:56
Ari	11	*22:49
Tau	14	*07:55
Gem	16	*15:05
Can	18	*20:00
Leo	20	*22:34
Vir	22	*23:29

1966		
Sag	23	*03:51
Cap	25	*11:37
Aqu	27	*21:56
Pis	30	*09:48
Ari	1	*22:27
Tau	4	*10:58
Gem	6	*21:51
Can	9	*05:26
Leo	11	*08:59
Vir	13	*09:25
Lib	15	*08:33
Sco	17	*08:34
Sag	19	*11:22
Cap	21	*17:52

1967		
Tau	25	*08:21
Gem	27	*21:07
Can	30	*07:33
Leo	1	*14:06
Vir	3	*17:07
Lib	5	*18:02
Sco	7	*18:44
Sag	9	*20:40
Cap	12	*00:43
Aqu	14	*07:08
Pis	16	*15:53
Ari	19	*02:46
Tau	21	*15:20

1968		
Vir	23	*22:20
Lib	26	*03:44
Sco	28	*07:38
Sag	30	*10:40
Cap	1	*13:21
Aqu	3	*16:19
Pis	5	*20:27
Ari	8	*02:49
Tau	10	*12:06
Gem	12	*23:54
Can	15	*12:27
Leo	17	*23:24
Vir	20	*07:15
Lib	22	*11:58

1969		
Cap	23	*02:48
Aqu	25	*03:35
Pis	27	*04:03
Ari	29	*05:57
Tau	31	*10:51
Gem	2	*19:23
Can	5	*06:56
Leo	7	*19:35
Vir	10	*07:20
Lib	12	*17:01
Sco	15	*00:24
Sag	17	*05:41
Cap	19	*09:13
Aqu	21	*11:30

♍ Virgo – Finding Your Moon Sign ☽

1970		
Gem	23	*20:04
Can	26	*04:58
Leo	28	*16:38
Vir	31	*05:35
Lib	2	*18:25
Sco	5	*05:54
Sag	7	*14:57
Cap	9	*20:50
Aqu	11	*23:32
Pis	13	*23:56
Ari	15	*23:35
Tau	18	*00:22
Gem	20	*04:02
Can	22	*11:41

1971		
Lib	23	*16:22
Sco	26	*05:08
Sag	28	*16:56
Cap	31	*01:53
Aqu	2	*07:03
Pis	4	*08:50
Ari	6	*08:43
Tau	8	*08:37
Gem	10	*10:25
Can	12	*15:21
Leo	14	*23:38
Vir	17	*10:29
Lib	19	*22:47
Sco	22	*11:32

1972		
Pis	24	*15:27
Ari	26	*18:40
Tau	28	*20:42
Gem	30	*22:55
Can	2	*02:11
Leo	4	*06:53
Vir	6	*13:15
Lib	8	*21:37
Sco	11	*08:15
Sag	13	*20:42
Cap	16	*09:06
Aqu	18	*19:04

1973		
Can	23	*16:07
Leo	25	*17:48
Vir	27	*19:33
Lib	29	*22:53
Sco	1	*05:17
Sag	3	*15:24
Cap	6	*04:00
Aqu	8	*16:30
Pis	11	*02:39
Ari	13	*09:55
Tau	15	*14:58
Gem	17	*18:47
Can	19	*22:00
Leo	22	*00:56

1974		
Sag	24	*13:35
Cap	27	*00:15
Aqu	29	*12:52
Pis	1	*01:28
Ari	3	*12:57
Tau	5	*22:49
Gem	8	*06:35
Can	10	*11:38
Leo	12	*13:53
Vir	14	*14:11
Lib	16	*14:17
Sco	18	*16:14
Sag	20	*21:47

♍ Virgo – Finding Your Moon Sign ☽

1975		
Ari	24	*12:02
Tau	27	*00:44
Gem	29	*11:52
Can	31	*19:34
Leo	2	*23:06
Vir	4	*23:28
Lib	6	*22:38
Sco	8	*22:46
Sag	11	*01:41
Cap	13	*08:11
Aqu	15	*17:51
Pis	18	*05:31
Ari	20	*18:06

1976		
Leo	23	*03:29
Vir	25	*07:03
Lib	27	*08:41
Sco	29	*10:05
Sag	31	*12:28
Cap	2	*16:29
Aqu	4	*22:20
Pis	7	*06:11
Ari	9	*16:18
Tau	12	*04:30
Gem	14	*17:32
Can	17	*05:06
Leo	19	*13:09
Vir	21	*17:15

1977		
Cap	24	*05:30
Aqu	26	*07:40
Pis	28	*10:47
Ari	30	*16:11
Tau	2	*00:52
Gem	4	*12:27
Can	7	*01:02
Leo	9	*12:12
Vir	11	*20:33
Lib	14	*02:06
Sco	16	*05:45
Sag	18	*08:28
Cap	20	*11:04
Aqu	22	*14:12

1978		
Tau	23	*00:06
Gem	25	*08:31
Can	27	*19:59
Leo	30	*08:39
Vir	1	*20:45
Lib	4	*07:15
Sco	6	*15:37
Sag	8	*21:38
Cap	11	*01:18
Aqu	13	*03:08
Pis	15	*04:09
Ari	17	*05:49
Tau	19	*09:43
Gem	21	*16:56

1979		
Lib	25	*08:13
Sco	27	*20:11
Sag	30	*05:39
Cap	1	*11:32
Aqu	3	*13:58
Pis	5	*14:02
Ari	7	*13:29
Tau	9	*14:13
Gem	11	*17:54
Can	14	*01:27
Leo	16	*12:25
Vir	19	*01:15
Lib	21	*14:10

♍ Virgo – Finding Your Moon Sign ☽

1980		
Aqu	23	*20:31
Pis	25	*22:42
Ari	27	*23:10
Tau	29	*23:41
Gem	1	*01:50
Can	3	*06:39
Leo	5	*14:22
Vir	8	*00:31
Lib	10	*12:22
Sco	13	*01:05
Sag	15	*13:27
Cap	17	*23:43
Aqu	20	*06:30
Pis	22	*09:26

1981		
Can	24	*18:16
Leo	26	*22:10
Vir	29	*03:32
Lib	31	*11:03
Sco	2	*21:10
Sag	5	*09:23
Cap	7	*21:47
Aqu	10	*07:57
Pis	12	*14:32
Ari	14	*17:55
Tau	16	*19:30
Gem	18	*20:59
Can	20	*23:40

1982		
Sco	23	*18:20
Sag	26	*04:11
Cap	28	*16:41
Aqu	31	*05:23
Pis	2	*16:10
Ari	5	*00:22
Tau	7	*06:26
Gem	9	*10:56
Can	11	*14:17
Leo	13	*16:45
Vir	15	*18:57
Lib	17	*22:03
Sco	20	*03:33
Sag	22	*12:31

1983		
Pis	23	*15:09
Ari	26	*03:07
Tau	28	*13:37
Gem	30	*21:47
Can	2	*02:51
Leo	4	*04:46
Vir	6	*04:35
Lib	8	*04:13
Sco	10	*05:49
Sag	12	*11:09
Cap	14	*20:34
Aqu	17	*08:45
Pis	19	*21:29
Ari	22	*09:09

1984		
Leo	24	*12:58
Vir	26	*13:31
Lib	28	*12:57
Sco	30	*13:24
Sag	1	*16:30
Cap	3	*22:55
Aqu	6	*08:11
Pis	8	*19:24
Ari	11	*07:46
Tau	13	*20:32
Gem	16	*08:25
Can	18	*17:35
Leo	20	*22:47

♍ Virgo – Finding Your Moon Sign ☽

1985		
Sag	23	*04:36
Cap	25	*08:24
Aqu	27	*13:31
Pis	29	*20:25
Ari	1	*05:41
Tau	3	*17:27
Gem	6	*06:26
Can	8	*18:10
Leo	11	*02:26
Vir	13	*06:52
Lib	15	*08:33
Sco	17	*09:17
Sag	19	*10:41
Cap	21	*13:49

1986		
Tau	24	*13:37
Gem	27	*01:00
Can	29	*13:39
Leo	1	*01:07
Vir	3	*10:04
Lib	5	*16:33
Sco	7	*21:11
Sag	10	*00:39
Cap	12	*03:27
Aqu	14	*06:06
Pis	16	*09:27
Ari	18	*14:34
Tau	20	*22:26

1987		
Vir	24	*10:22
Lib	26	*21:34
Sco	29	*06:48
Sag	31	*13:22
Cap	2	*17:03
Aqu	4	*18:21
Pis	6	*18:36
Ari	8	*19:34
Tau	10	*22:58
Gem	13	*05:54
Can	15	*16:22
Leo	18	*04:50
Vir	20	*17:12

1988		
Cap	23	*01:47
Aqu	25	*04:04
Pis	27	*04:00
Ari	29	*03:29
Tau	31	*04:22
Gem	2	*08:11
Can	4	*15:37
Leo	7	*02:14
Vir	9	*14:47
Lib	12	*03:50
Sco	14	*16:06
Sag	17	*02:24
Cap	19	*09:43
Aqu	21	*13:41

1989		
Gem	23	*17:38
Can	25	*22:13
Leo	28	*05:11
Vir	30	*14:29
Lib	2	*01:47
Sco	4	*14:23
Sag	7	*02:50
Cap	9	*13:11
Aqu	11	*20:00
Pis	13	*23:06
Ari	15	*23:37
Tau	17	*23:22
Gem	20	*00:16
Can	22	*03:51

♍ Virgo – Finding Your Moon Sign ☽

1990

Lib	23	*00:17
Sco	25	*09:56
Sag	27	*21:57
Cap	30	*10:22
Aqu	1	*20:50
Pis	4	*04:04
Ari	6	*08:22
Tau	8	*10:55
Gem	10	*13:04
Can	12	*15:52
Leo	14	*19:52
Vir	17	*01:19
Lib	19	*08:34
Sco	21	*18:05

1991

Pis	25	*05:51
Ari	27	*15:00
Tau	29	*21:58
Gem	1	*03:01
Can	3	*06:19
Leo	5	*08:12
Vir	7	*09:35
Lib	9	*11:52
Sco	11	*16:42
Sag	14	*01:15
Cap	16	*13:03
Aqu	19	*01:57
Pis	21	*13:19

1992

Can	23	*17:36
Leo	25	*19:14
Vir	27	*18:46
Lib	29	*18:10
Sco	31	*19:39
Sag	3	*00:51
Cap	5	*10:06
Aqu	7	*22:08
Pis	10	*10:55
Ari	12	*23:01
Tau	15	*09:46
Gem	17	*18:39
Can	20	*00:57
Leo	22	*04:18

1993

Sag	24	*07:45
Cap	26	*13:58
Aqu	28	*22:42
Pis	31	*09:18
Ari	2	*21:20
Tau	5	*10:09
Gem	7	*22:15
Can	10	*07:35
Leo	12	*12:49
Vir	14	*14:19
Lib	16	*13:43
Sco	18	*13:15
Sag	20	*14:54
Cap	22	*19:54

1994

Ari	23	*18:54
Tau	26	*06:13
Gem	28	*19:07
Can	31	*06:59
Leo	2	*15:36
Vir	4	*20:32
Lib	6	*22:56
Sco	9	*00:25
Sag	11	*02:25
Cap	13	*05:44
Aqu	15	*10:42
Pis	17	*17:31
Ari	20	*02:30
Tau	22	*13:47

♍ Virgo – Finding Your Moon Sign ☽

1995		
Leo	23	*14:11
Vir	25	*23:49
Lib	28	*07:14
Sco	30	*12:50
Sag	1	*16:56
Cap	3	*19:44
Aqu	5	*21:47
Pis	8	*00:08
Ari	10	*04:14
Tau	12	*11:22
Gem	14	*21:48
Can	17	*10:15
Leo	19	*22:18
Vir	22	*08:00

1996		
Cap	24	*08:21
Aqu	26	*09:09
Pis	28	*08:48
Ari	30	*09:15
Tau	1	*12:20
Gem	3	*19:08
Can	6	*05:29
Leo	8	*17:53
Vir	11	*06:28
Lib	13	*17:50
Sco	16	*03:19
Sag	18	*10:29
Cap	20	*15:11
Aqu	22	*17:39

1997		
Gem	24	*22:57
Can	27	*06:10
Leo	29	*16:18
Vir	1	*04:26
Lib	3	*17:29
Sco	6	*06:09
Sag	8	*16:53
Cap	11	*00:21
Aqu	13	*04:09
Pis	15	*04:58
Ari	17	*04:24
Tau	19	*04:21
Gem	21	*06:38

1998		
Lib	24	*15:02
Sco	27	*03:25
Sag	29	*15:54
Cap	1	*02:21
Aqu	3	*09:19
Pis	5	*12:46
Ari	7	*13:52
Tau	9	*14:16
Gem	11	*15:40
Can	13	*19:20
Leo	16	*01:48
Vir	18	*10:52
Lib	20	*21:57

1999		
Aqu	24	*09:48
Pis	26	*17:49
Ari	28	*23:08
Tau	31	*02:40
Gem	2	*05:24
Can	4	*08:09
Leo	6	*11:29
Vir	8	*15:56
Lib	10	*22:16
Sco	13	*07:08
Sag	15	*18:34
Cap	18	*07:13
Aqu	20	*18:37

2000		
Can	24	*21:58
Leo	26	*23:16
Vir	28	*23:55
Lib	31	*01:33
Sco	2	*05:54
Sag	4	*14:09
Cap	7	*01:47
Aqu	9	*14:44
Pis	12	*02:33
Ari	14	*11:59
Tau	16	*19:04
Gem	19	*00:21
Can	21	*04:15

₥ Virgo Mercury Signs ☿

DATES	LEO	VIRGO	LIBRA
1930		23 Aug–26 Aug	26 Aug–20 Sep
		20 Sep–23 Sep	
1931		23 Aug–23 Sep	
1932		23 Aug–9 Sep	9 Sep–23 Sep
1933	23 Aug–2 Sep	2 Sep–18 Sep	18 Sep–23 Sep
1934	23 Aug–25 Aug	25 Aug–10 Sep	10 Sep–23 Sep
1935		23 Aug–3 Sep	3 Sep–23 Sep
1936		23 Aug–27 Aug	27 Aug–23 Sep
1937		23 Aug–23 Sep	
1938	3 Sep–10 Sep	23 Aug–3 Sep	
		10 Sep–23 Sep	
1939	23 Aug–7 Sep	7 Sep–23 Sep	
1940	23 Aug–29 Aug	29 Aug–14 Sep	14 Sep–23 Sep
1941		23 Aug–6 Sep	6 Sep–23 Sep
1942		23 Aug–31 Aug	31 Aug–23 Sep
1943		23 Aug–27 Aug	27 Aug–23 Sep
1944		23 Aug–23 Sep	
1945	23 Aug–10 Sep	10 Sep–23 Sep	
1946	23 Aug–3 Sep	3 Sep–19 Sep	19 Sep–23 Sep
1947	23 Aug–26 Aug	26 Aug–11 Sep	11 Sep–23 Sep
1948		23 Aug–3 Sep	3 Sep–23 Sep
1949		23 Aug–28 Aug	28 Aug–23 Sep
1950		23 Aug–27 Aug	27 Aug–10 Sep
		10 Sep–23 Sep	
1951		23 Aug–23 Sep	
1952	23 Aug–7 Sep	7 Sep–23 Sep	23 Sep
1953	23 Aug–30 Aug	30 Aug–15 Sep	15 Sep–23 Sep
1954		23 Aug–8 Sep	8 Sep–23 Sep
1955		23 Aug–1 Sep	1 Sep–23 Sep

DATES	LEO	VIRGO	LIBRA
1956		23 Aug–26 Aug	26 Aug–23 Sep
1957		23 Aug–23 Sep	
1958	23 Aug–11 Sep	23 Aug	
		11 Sep–23 Sep	
1959	23 Aug–5 Sep	5 Sep–21 Sep	21 Sep–23 Sep
1960	23 Aug–27 Aug	27 Aug–12 Sep	12 Sep–23 Sep
1961		23 Aug–4 Sep	4 Sep–23 Sep
1962		23 Aug–29 Aug	29 Aug–23 Sep
1963		23 Aug–26 Aug	26 Aug–16 Sep
		16 Sep–23 Sep	
1964		23 Aug–23 Sep	
1965	23 Aug–8 Sep	8 Sep–23 Sep	
1966	23 Aug–1 Sep	1 Sep–17 Sep	17 Sep–23 Sep
1967	23 Aug–24 Aug	24 Aug–9 Sep	9 Sep–23 Sep
1968		23 Aug–1 Sep	1 Sep–23 Sep
1969		23 Aug–27 Aug	27 Aug–23 Sep
1970		23 Aug–23 Sep	
1971	23 Aug–29 Aug	29 Aug–11 Sep	11 Sep–23 Sep
1972	23 Aug–5 Sep	5 Sep–21 Sep	21 Sep–23 Sep
1973	23 Aug–28 Aug	28 Aug–13 Sep	13 Sep–23 Sep
1974		23 Aug–6 Sep	6 Sep–23 Sep
1975		23 Aug–30 Aug	30 Aug–23 Sep
1976		23 Aug–25 Aug	25 Aug–23 Sep
1977		23 Aug–-23 Sep	
1978	23 Aug–9 Sep	9 Sep–23 Sep	
1979	23 Aug–2 Sep	2 Sep–18 Sep	18 Sep–23 Sep
1980	23 Aug–24 Aug	24 Aug–10 Sep	10 Sep–23 Sep
1981		23 Aug–2 Sep	2 Sep–23 Sep
1982		23 Aug–28 Aug	28 Aug–23 Sep
1983		23 Aug–29 Aug	29 Aug–6 Sep
		6 Sep–23 Sep	
1984		23 Aug–23 Sep	

DATES	LEO	VIRGO	LIBRA
1985	23 Aug–6 Sep	6 Sep–23 Sep	
1986	23 Aug–30 Aug	30 Aug–15 Sep	15 Sep–23 Sep
1987		23 Aug–7 Sep	7 Sep–23 Sep
1988		23 Aug–7 Sep	7 Sep–23 Sep
1989		23 Aug–26 Aug	26 Aug–23 Sep
1990		23 Aug–23 Sep	
1991	23 Aug–10 Sep	10 Sep–23 Sep	
1992	23 Aug–3 Sep	3 Sep–19 Sep	19 Sep–23 Sep
1993	23 Aug–26 Aug	26 Aug–11 Sep	11 Sep–23 Sep
1994		23 Aug–4 Sep	4 Sep–23 Sep
1995		23 Aug–29 Aug	29 Aug–23 Sep
1996		23 Aug–26 Aug	26 Aug–12 Sep
		12 Sep–23 Sep	
1997		23 Aug–23 Sep	
1998	23 Aug–8 Sep	8 Sep–23 Sep	
1999	23 Aug–31 Aug	31 Aug–16 Sep	16 Sep–23 Sep
2000		23 Aug–7 Sep	7 Sep–23 Sep

♍ Virgo Venus Signs ♀

YEAR	CANCER	LEO	VIRGO	LIBRA	SCORPIO
1930		23 Aug–27 Aug	27 Aug–20 Sep	20 Sep–23 Sep	
1931	23 Aug–8 Sep	8 Sep–23 Sep			
1932				23 Aug–7 Sep	7 Sep–23 Sep
1933		23 Aug–11 Sep	11 Sep–23 Sep		
1934			23 Aug–23 Sep		
1935				23 Aug–15 Sep	15 Sep–23 Sep
1936	23 Aug–31 Aug	31 Aug– 23 Sep			
1937			23 Aug–4 Sep	4 Sep–23 Sep	
1938		23 Aug–26 Aug	26 Sug–20 Sep	20 Sep–23 Sep	
1939	23 Aug–8 Sep	8 Sep–23 Sep			
1940				23 Aug–7 Sep	7 Sep–23 Sep
1941		23 Aug–10 Sep	10 Sep–23 Sep		
1942			23 Aug–23 Sep		
1943				23 Aug–15 Sep	15 Sep–23 Sep
1944	23 Aug–30 Aug	30 Aug–23 Sep			
1945			23 Aug–3 Sep	3 Sep–23 Sep	
1946		23 Aug–26 Aug	26 Aug–19 Sep	19 Sep–23 Sep	
1947	23 Aug–8 Sep	8 Sep–23 Sep			
1948				23 Aug–7 Sep	7 Sep–23 Sep
1949		23 Aug–10 Sep	10 Sep–23 Sep		
1950			23 Aug–23 Sep		
1951				23 Aug–14 Sep	14 Sep–23 Sep

YEAR	CANCER	LEO	VIRGO	LIBRA	SCORPIO
1952	23 Aug–30 Aug	30 Aug–23 Sep	23 Aug–3 Sep	3 Sep–23 Sep	
1953				23 Aug–6 Sep	6 Sep–23 Sep
1954		23 Aug–25 Aug	25 Aug–18 Sep	18 Sep–23 Sep	
1955	23 Aug–8 Sep	8 Sep–23 Sep			
1956				23 Aug–14 Sep	14 Sep–23 Sep
1957					
1958		23 Aug–9 Sep	9 Sep–23 Sep		
1959			23 Aug–20 Sep	20 Sep–23 Sep	
1960			23 Aug–2 Sep	2 Sep–23 Sep	
1961	23 Aug–29 Aug	29 Aug–23 Sep			
1962				23 Aug–7 Sep	7 Sep–23 Sep
1963		23 Aug–25 Aug	25 Aug–18 Sep	18 Sep–23 Sep	
1964	23 Aug–8 Sep	8 Sep–23 Sep			
1965				23 Aug–13 Sep	13 Sep–23 Sep
1966		23 Aug–8 Sep	8 Sep–23 Sep		
1967			23 Aug–9 Sep	9 Sep–23 Sep	
1968			23 Aug–2 Sep	2 Sep–23 Sep	
1969	23 Aug–29 Aug	29 Aug–23 Sep			
1970				23 Aug–7 Sep	7 Sep–23 Sep
1971		23 Aug–24 Aug	24 Aug–17 Sep	17 Sep–23 Sep	
1972	23 Aug–7 Sep	7 Sep–23 Sep			
1973				23 Aug–13 Sep	13 Sep–23 Sep
1974		23 Aug–8 Sep	8 Sep–23 Sep		
1975		2 Sep–23 Sep	23 Aug–2 Sep		
1976			23 Aug–1 Sep	1 Sep–23 Sep	

YEAR	CANCER	LEO	VIRGO	LIBRA	SCORPIO
1977	23 Aug–28 Aug	28 Aug–23 Sep	23 Sep	23 Aug–7 Sep	
1978				17 Sep–23 Sep	7 Sep–23 Sep
1979		23 Aug–24 Aug	24 Aug–17 Sep		
1980	23 Aug–7 Sep	7 Sep–23 Sep		23 Aug–12 Sep	12 Sep–23 Sep
1981					
1982		23 Aug–7 Sep	7 Sep–23 Sep	27 Aug–23 Sep	
1983			23 Aug–27 Aug	1 Sep–23 Sep	
1984			23 Aug–1 Sep		
1985	23 Aug–28 Aug	28 Aug–23 Sep	23 Sep		
1986				23 Aug–7 Sep	7 Sep–23 Sep
1987		23 Aug	23 Aug–16 Sep	16 Sep–23 Sep	
1988	23 Aug–7 Sep	7 Sep–23 Sep			
1989				23 Aug–12 Sep	12 Sep–23 Sep
1990		23 Aug–7 Sep	7 Sep–23 Sep		
1991		23 Aug–23 Sep			
1992			23 Aug–31 Aug	31 Aug–23 Sep	
1993	23 Aug–27 Aug	27 Aug–23 Sep			
1994				23 Aug–7 Sep	7 Sep–23 Sep
1995		23 Aug	23 Aug–16 Sep	16 Sep–23 Sep	
1996	23 Aug–7 Sep	7 Sep–23 Sep			
1997				23 Aug–12 Sep	12 Sep–23 Sep
1998		23 Aug–6 Sep	6 Sep–23 Sep		
1999		23 Aug–23 Sep			
2000			22 Aug–31 Aug	31 Aug–23 Sep	

The Virgo Workbook

There are no right or wrong answers in this chapter. Its aim is to help you assess how you are doing with your life – in YOUR estimation – and to make the material of this book more personal and, I hope, more helpful for you.

1.The Virgo in You
Which of the following Virgo characteristics do you recognise in yourself?

analytical	competent	discriminating
efficient	hard-working	meticulous
modest	orderly	precise
resourceful	skilful	clever

2. In which situations do you find yourself acting like this?

_____

_____

3. When you are feeling vulnerable, you may show some of the less constructive Virgo traits. Do you recognise yourself in any of the following?

uptight	nit-picking	stingy
fault-finding	finicky	know-it-all
workaholic	highly strung	petty-minded

What kind of situations trigger off this behaviour and what do you think might help you, in these situations, to respond more positively?

_____

_____

4. You and Your Roles
a) Where, if anywhere, in your life do you play the role of Craftsman or Craftswoman?

_____

_____

b) What do you craft?

_____

_____

5. Do you play any of the following roles – in the literal or broad sense – in any part of your life? If not, would you like to? What might be your first step towards doing so?

Analyst	Critic	Fixer
Server	Purifier	Bringer of Order

_____

_____

6. Sun Aspects
If any of the following planets aspects your Sun, add each of the keywords for that planet to complete the following sentences. Which phrases ring true for you?

I am _____

My father is _____

My job requires that I am _____

Saturn Words (Use only if your Sun is aspected by Saturn)

ambitious	controlling	judgmental	mature
serious	strict	traditional	bureaucratic
cautious	committed	hard-working	disciplined
depressive	responsible	status-seeking	limiting

Uranus Words (Use only if your Sun is aspected by Uranus)

freedom-loving	progressive	rebellious	shocking
scientific	cutting-edge	detached	contrary
friendly	disruptive	eccentric	humanitarian
innovative	nonconformist	unconventional	exciting

Neptune Words (Use only if your Sun is aspected by Neptune)

sensitive	idealistic	artistic	impressionable
disappointing	impractical	escapist	self-sacrificing
spiritual	unrealistic	dreamy	glamorous
dependent	deceptive	rescuing	blissful

Pluto Words (Use only if your Sun is aspected by Pluto)

powerful	single-minded	intense	extreme
secretive	rotten	passionate	mysterious
investigative	uncompromising	ruthless	wealthy
abusive	regenerative	associated with sex, birth or death	

a) If one or more negative words describe you or your job, how might you turn that quality into something more positive or satisfying?

_____

_____

7. The Moon and You

Below are brief lists of what the Moon needs, in the various elements, to feel secure and satisfied. First find your Moon element, then estimate how much of each of the following you are expressing and receiving in your life, especially at home and in your relationships, on a scale of 0 to 5 where 0 = none and 5 = plenty.

FIRE MOONS — Aries, Leo, Sagittarius

attention	action	drama
recognition	self-expression	spontaneity
enthusiasm	adventure	leadership

EARTH MOONS — Taurus, Virgo, Capricorn

stability	orderly routine	sensual pleasures
material security	a sense of rootedness	control over your home life
regular body care	practical achievements	pleasurable practical tasks

AIR MOONS — Gemini, Libra, Aquarius

mental rapport	stimulating ideas	emotional space
friendship	social justice	interesting conversations
fairness	socialising	freedom to circulate

WATER MOONS — Cancer, Scorpio, Pisces

intimacy	a sense of belonging	emotional rapport
emotional safety	respect for your feelings	time and space to retreat
acceptance	cherishing and being cherished	warmth and comfort

a) Do you feel your Moon is being 'fed' enough?
yes_____   no_____

b) How might you satisfy your Moon needs even better?

_____

_____

8. You and Your Mercury

As a Virgo, your Mercury can only be in Leo, Virgo or Libra. Below are some of the ways and situations in which Mercury in each of the elements might learn and communicate effectively. First find your Mercury sign, then circle the words you think apply to you.

Mercury in Fire (Leo)

action	imagination	identifying with the subject matter
excitement	drama	playing with possibilities

Mercury in Earth (Virgo)

time-tested methods	useful facts	well-structured information
'how to' instructions	demonstrations	hands-on experience

Mercury in Air (Libra)

facts arranged in categories	logic	demonstrable connections
rational arguments	theories	debate and sharing of ideas

Mercury in Water (As a Virgo you can never have Mercury in a water sign; the words are included here for completeness)

pictures and images	charged atmospheres	feeling-linked information
intuitive understanding	emotional rapport	being shown personally

a) This game with Mercury can be done with a friend or on

your own. Skim through a magazine until you find a picture that interests you. Then describe the picture – to your friend, or in writing or on tape. Notice what you emphasise and the kind of words you use. Now try to describe it using the language and emphasis of each of the other Mercury modes. How easy did you find that? Identifying the preferred Mercury style of others and using that style yourself can lead to improved communication all round.

9. Your Venus Values
Below are lists of qualities and situations that your Venus sign might enjoy. Assess on a scale of 0 to 5 how much your Venus desires and pleasures are met and expressed in your life. 0 = not at all, 5 = fully.

Venus in Cancer
You will activate your Venus through anything that makes you feel wise, intuitive, nurturing and nurtured, and at the centre of a 'family', for example:

a beautiful home	tenderness	sharing meals with loved ones
sharing feelings safely	home comforts	your family or country history

Venus in Leo
You will activate your Venus through anything that makes you feel special, unique, radiant and generous, for example:

extravagant gestures	luxury goods	prestigious activities
being central in a drama	acting nobly	being in love

Venus in Virgo

You will activate your Venus through anything that engages your powers of discrimination, for example:

restoring order	improving efficiency	using your skills
purifying your mind, body or environment	being of service	quality work

Venus in Libra

You will activate your Venus through anything cultured, balanced and fair, for example:

harmonious relationships	elegant surroundings	dressing well
courteous manners	artistic pursuits	political justice

Venus in Scorpio

You will activate your Venus through anything that allows you to penetrate to the heart of life's mysteries, for example:

survival situations	money, power or sex	investigating secrets
transformative experiences	recycling	intense relationships

a) How, and where, might you have more fun and pleasure by bringing more of what your Venus sign loves into your life?

_____

_____

b) Make a note here of the kind of gifts your Venus sign would love to receive. Then go on and spoil yourself . . .

_____

_____

Resources

Finding an Astrologer

I'm often asked what is the best way to find a reputable astrologer. Personal recommendation by someone whose judgement you trust is by far the best way. Ideally, the astrologer should also be endorsed by a reputable organisation whose members adhere to a strict code of ethics, which guarantees confidentiality and professional conduct.

Contact Addresses

Association of Professional Astrologers International
www.professionalastrologers.org
   APAI members adhere to a strict code of professional ethics.

Astrological Association of Great Britain
www.astrologicalassociation.co.uk
   The main body for astrology in the UK, with links to similar organisations throughout the world.

Faculty of Astrological Studies
www.astrology.org.uk
   The teaching body internationally recognised for excellence in astrological education at all levels.

Jane Ridder-Patrick
www.janeridderpatrick.com

Your Virgo Friends

You can keep a record of Virgos you know here, with the page numbers of where to find their descriptions handy for future reference.

Name _____ Date of Birth _____

Aspects*	None	Saturn	Uranus	Neptune	Pluto
Moon Sign _____				p _____	
Mercury Sign _____				p _____	
Venus Sign _____				p _____	

Name _____ Date of Birth _____

Aspects*	None	Saturn	Uranus	Neptune	Pluto
Moon Sign _____				p _____	
Mercury Sign _____				p _____	
Venus Sign _____				p _____	

Name _____ Date of Birth _____

Aspects*	None	Saturn	Uranus	Neptune	Pluto
Moon Sign _____				p _____	
Mercury Sign _____				p _____	
Venus Sign _____				p _____	

Name _____ Date of Birth _____

Aspects*	None	Saturn	Uranus	Neptune	Pluto
Moon Sign _____				p _____	
Mercury Sign _____				p _____	
Venus Sign _____				p _____	

* Circle where applicable

Sign Summaries

SIGN	GLYPH	APPROX DATES	SYMBOL	ROLE	ELEMENT	QUALITY	PLANET	GLYPH	KEYWORD
1. Aries	♈	21/3 – 19/4	Ram	Hero	Fire	Cardinal	Mars	♂	Assertiveness
2. Taurus	♉	20/4 – 20/5	Bull	Steward	Earth	Fixed	Venus	♀	Stability
3. Gemini	♊	21/5 – 21/6	Twins	Go-Between	Air	Mutable	Mercury	☿	Communication
4. Cancer	♋	22/6 – 22/7	Crab	Caretaker	Water	Cardinal	Moon	☽	Nurture
5. Leo	♌	23/7 – 22/8	Lion	Performer	Fire	Fixed	Sun	☉	Glory
6. Virgo	♍	23/8 – 22/9	Maiden	Craftworker	Earth	Mutable	Mercury	☿	Skill
7. Libra	♎	23/9 – 22/10	Scales	Architect	Air	Cardinal	Venus	♀	Balance
8. Scorpio	♏	23/10 – 23/11	Scorpion	Survivor	Water	Fixed	Pluto	♇	Transformation
9. Sagittarius	♐	22/11 – 21/12	Archer	Adventurer	Fire	Mutable	Jupiter	♃	Wisdom
10. Capricorn	♑	22/12 – 19/1	Goat	Manager	Earth	Cardinal	Saturn	♄	Responsibility
11. Aquarius	♒	20/1 – 19/2	Waterbearer	Scientist	Air	Fixed	Uranus	♅	Progress
12. Pisces	♓	20/2 – 20/3	Fishes	Dreamer	Water	Mutable	Neptune	♆	Universality